feng shui in the home

Creating Harmony in the Home

feng shui in the home

Creating Harmony in the Home

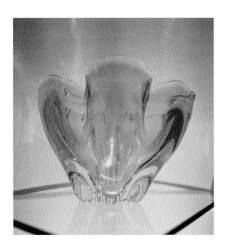

Siobhan O'Brien
Photography: Brett Boardman

PERIPLUS

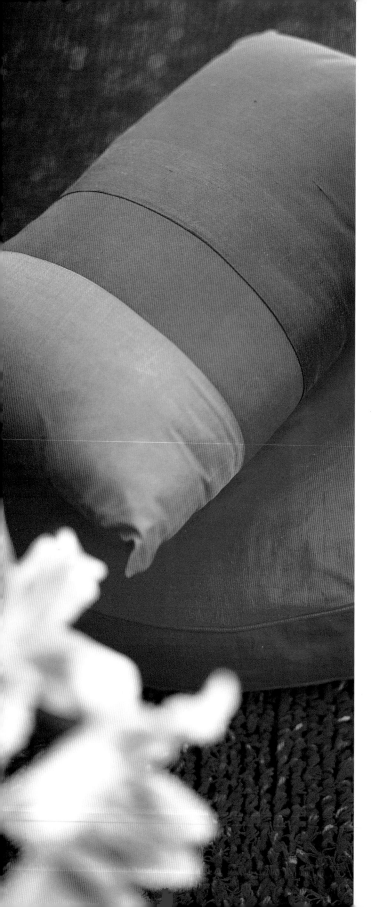

AD is referred to in the text as CE (Common Era)
BC is referred to in the text as BCE (Before Common Era)

First published in the United States in 2002 by Periplus Editions (HK) Lt
with editorial offices at 153 Milk Street, Boston, Massachusetts 02109 a
130 Joo Seng Road #06-01/03 Singapore 368357

Library of Congress Cataloging-in-Publication Data is available.
ISBN 0-7946-5015-5

DISTRIBUTED BY

North America, Latin America, and Europe
Tuttle Publishing
Distribution Center
Airport Industrial Park
364 Innovation Drive
North Clarendon
VT 05759-9436
Tel: (802) 773-8930
Tel: (800) 526-2778

Japan and Korea
Tuttle Publishing
Yaekari Bldg., 3rd Floor
5-4-12 Osaki
Shinagawa-ku
Tokyo 141-0032
Tel: (03) 5437-0171
Fax: (03) 5437-0755

Asia Pacific
Berkeley Books Pte. L
130 Joo Seng Road
#06-01/03
Singapore 368357
Tel: (65) 6280-3320
Fax: (65) 6280-6290

Commissioned by Deborah Nixon
Text: Siobhan O'Brien
Photography: Brett Boardman
Styling: Kathy McKinnon
Stylist's assistant: Imogen Carr
Illustration: Jane Cameron
Design: Robyn Latimer
Copy Editor: Sarah Shrubb
Production Manager: Sally Stokes
Project Coordinator: Kate Merrifield

First Edition
06 05 04 03 02 01   10 9 8 7 6 5 4 3 2 1

Set in Gill Sans, Officina Sans, Ruling Script
and Trebuchet on QuarkXPress
Printed in Singapore

Contents

A Celebration of the Everyday

Right: According to the ancient Chinese tradition of Feng Shui, applying a positive image, such as this image of a flower, is a powerful tool for activating or enhancing life aspirations such as prosperity, romance, or fame and acknowledgment. Other positive images include landscapes, festivities or groups of friends, which are thought to generate abundance in the related life sector. Combining this principle and good design practice, such as a square or rectangular room, will greatly assist with the energy flow in the home.

Below: Double figures or objects act as Feng Shui enhancers within the home for romance, friendship or support – depending on which aspect of your life you wish to activate. But remember, the ancient art of Feng Shui is not about objects themselves; it is about how consciously and sensitively the objects are placed. It teaches us to implement, position and utilize objects not purely as aesthetic items, but rather as things which have the capacity to enhance our lives.

This book makes some assumptions. You work hard, you're time poor. Your home environment is important. You have a sense of style. And you love beautiful things. But you're also interested in different ways of living and restoring balance within your life.

Balance doesn't come easy. It's about looking within and shifting our focus – from deadlines, making money and racing the clock to seeking ways to bring out the best in ourselves, in others and in the environment in which we live. Balance is about living artfully, consciously, and joyously celebrating the everyday. It's about caring, taking time, living in the moment. Everything we do, and the willingness with which we do it, provides us with an opportunity to live more fully – from how we live, how we arrange our homes and how we work to how we cook, how we tend our gardens, how we interact with others. The art of Feng Shui provides us with one of those opportunities.

The problem is, so many texts on this ancient Chinese philosophy are written in a language difficult to grasp, with a context that does not relate easily to our modern lifestyle. Equally, books on design can be elitist, targeting an "in-the-know" crowd. *Feng Shui in the Home: Creating Harmony* is intended to be accessible and practical, without straying from underlying foundations or principles of Feng Shui.

Fundamentally, what sets Feng Shui apart from other philosophical systems is that it can be integrated into any culture, alongside any belief system. So it's possible for each of us to apply materials, forms, objects and colors from our own society, traditions and background in our use of Feng Shui. But Feng Shui is about utilising and implementing the objects around us, not just as aesthetic items, but as things which enhance our lives. It enables us to place ourselves in our environment to our best advantage. This phenomenon extends to concern for our environment and ways to avoid or minimize the damage and pollution we inflict on it.

The Basics

What is Feng Shui?

Feng Shui – commonly accepted as stemming from the Chinese Feng, the force of the wind, and Shui, the flow of water – is based on the theory that energy from these natural forces can be manipulated to flow beneficially. In classical texts, however, it is described as "tian ling di li ren he," which translates literally as "auspicious heavenly influence, beneficial topography, harmonious human actions." This description is more apt, as Feng Shui is a complex blend of astronomy, astrology, topography and science combined with the more human – social, societal, and cultural.

Most ancient systems evolved similarly – from an understanding or interpretation of the natural world, where natural phenomena such as lightning, storms, or droughts were thought to be imbued with a spirit or deity. Where these systems became religions, the deities were worshipped. Feng Shui, though, is not about worship; it's about the force of destiny or fate. It uses formulas to determine the rising and falling energy for an individual or a dwelling in a given time span. Other formulas indicate the best location or position for a person's home or office, and suggest the appropriate placement of beds, desks, seating arrangements, design schemes. It helps us determine which colors, layouts, designs, shapes, materials and plants will support and nurture us. Although there are some basic principles to follow in Feng Shui, it is a philosophy which understands our homes are direct extensions of ourselves; they are mirrors reflecting who we are.

The history of Feng Shui

Feng Shui is used today to orient the homes of the living, but in its earliest form it was used to orient the homes of the dead. In early Chinese history, appropriate and auspicious locations were determined by direction, astronomy and geophysical factors. Using the same methods, efficient agricultural systems were also created. The practice is as old as Chinese culture itself, dating back to Neolithic Yangshao villages (6000 BCE). The term "Feng Shui" first appeared in a passage from the *Book of Burial*, which dates to the 4th century CE.

Until recently, much of the literature on Feng Shui has only been available in Chinese, and its principles were largely unknown in the West. In its heady

Below: The principles of Feng Shui are evidenced in the position, direction and placement of ancient Chinese temples, buildings, burial sites, landscaping – even cities. The placement of structures within the natural world forms the basis of many of the oldest Feng Shui schools of thought. Here, an ornate detail on concrete stairs in a Chinese garden echoes shapes derived from nature, such as the wind, water or undulating hills. While also protecting the garden from the elements, due to it's solid shape, these stairs allow for the free flow of Qi and interconnection within the landscape.

days during the Tang Dynasty (618–907 CE), Feng Shui was confined to the ruling classes – to the emperor and his ministers. Court advisers had to pass imperial examinations which involved acquiring a profound knowledge of classical Chinese texts, which themselves were submerged in archaic language and symbolic explanations. One of these was the *I Ching* – known in the West as the *Book of Changes*. An important component of this book is knowledge of Feng Shui.

The ambitious within the court were required to be skilled in interpreting the divinations and predictions revealed in the *I Ching*. Those who acquired this knowledge enjoyed privileged positions. They were consulted when palaces and tombs were built and new cities were planned. They rigorously studied landscapes, calculated compass directions and diagnosed the positioning of buildings within land sites. They worked out appropriate dimensions for new buildings, and even investigated individual birth dates, to ensure that human energy could be harmoniously aligned to the home, residents and environments. This is essentially what Feng Shui masters and practitioners are doing today.

Opposite: Most early belief systems evolved from an interpretation and tribal understanding of the natural world. Natural phenomena, including sunsets, floods, lightning, storms, droughts or fire, were believed to be imbued with a spirit or deity. If there was a flood for example, it was thought the spirit was angry, or when the rain came it was thought to be a gift. Where these systems became religions, the deities were worshipped. Feng Shui is not about worship – it's about the forces of destiny or fate.

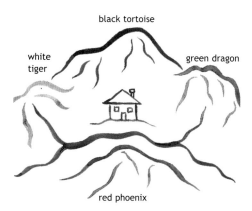

black tortoise

white tiger

green dragon

red phoenix

Above: The directions of the compass are symbolized by four mythical animals or spirits. The Red Phoenix marks the front boundary; the Black Tortoise the protective hill at the back; and the White Tiger and the Green Dragon, one on each side, offer protection from the wind – the dragon should be positioned slightly higher than the tiger. The "perfect arrangement" for a house has an open space in front, with the four celestial animals surrounding it for protection.

Above: The Form School of Feng Shui focuses on the contours of the physical landscape – shape, size, and position – and the relationship between these natural formations and buildings. As outlined above, the best plot of land has the four mythical animals surrounding it – where one is missing it is believed that large trees, rocks, a fence or a wall can be implemented to "substitute" the missing animal. To avoid such an imbalance in this backyard, large boulders and trees have been used to protect the occupants of the house.

Schools of Thought

A generic form of Feng Shui doesn't exist. Instead, a number of different approaches interpret environments, but they all focus on connecting with the energy of a place. Some schools of thought investigate living and working spaces with respect to their orientation to the magnetic field of the Earth. Other schools concentrate on the symbolism of terrain and intuition. Each of the various schools of thought, however, ends up with the same result. There's the Black Hat Sect School, a hybrid of Tibetan Buddhism, Taoism and Feng Shui. And the Flying Star School, where practitioners believe that over time the luck of any dwelling will change according to intangible forces, and Intuitive Feng Shui, with devices more familiar to our modern Western lifestyle. The most widely used schools are the Form and Compass Schools. Initially, the doctrines of these two schools developed independently, but today their difference is no longer very apparent.

The Form School

Sensibilities of ancient people living and working on the land were finely tuned, and their knowledge of the natural world endowed them with an instinct for suitable sites to grow their crops.

The Form School, the oldest school of Feng Shui, focuses on the contours of the physical landscape – shape, size and position – and the relationship between these natural formations and buildings. The four compass directions are symbolized by four celestial animals, representing the perfect arrangement. Feng Shui masters believe that the four entities must be present for a building to be prosperous. The ideal location for a house is Xue (pronounced Shu) – it has an open space in front known as the "Bright Hall" or "Ming Tang," and the four mythical animals surround it. The Red Phoenix marks the front boundary, the Black Tortoise marks the protective hill at the back, and the White Tiger and Green Dragon to each side offer protection from the wind, with the dragon positioned slightly higher than the tiger.

A stream or water flowing across the front of a site is good Feng Shui, as it represents food, transportation and trade. It is also believed that in this auspicious location the descending heaven Qi meets the ascending Qi (see page 14).

The Compass School

An ancient, formula-driven approach, the Compass School concerns itself with the magnetic effect of the Earth's gravitational fields. It relies on complex calculations, using the symbolic associations of the *I Ching* and the directions of the compass.

Forming the outer ring of the Bagua (see page 25), an eight-sided symbol, are eight symbolic trigrams, to which ancient sages added their wisdom in areas such as astrology, astronomy, science and geography over the centuries. These trigrams have corresponding attributes, symbols, colors, specific compass directions, even referring to different members of the family. Good or bad Feng Shui is determined by the placement of the trigrams around the Bagua. Interpreting their various energies suggests suitable sites for human beings.

The Lo Shu Magic Square and the Luo Pan (or compass) are additional tools used to determine the location and quality of Qi flow. In ancient China, geomancers investigated earth formations and watercourses, while astronomers charted the skies. Those who understood the power of the information recorded their knowledge on an instrument called a Luo Pan, which illustrates direction and investigates the energy of each direction. Forming the outer ring of the Luo Pan are 64 images from the yearly nature cycle, derived from the ancient text the *I Ching*.

Below: The Luo Pan (or compass) is an elaborate reference compass that contains all the signs and symbols which indicate auspicious or inauspicious Feng Shui. Images from the yearly nature cycle, derived from the ancient text the *I Ching*, illustrate the energy of each direction and offer clues for designing the interiors or exteriors of a home or building or for selecting a site.

Above: The purpose of Feng Shui is to create environments in which Qi flows freely. Where beneficial Qi (Sheng Qi) meanders gently along curved lines through the interiors of a home, the occupants will feel positive, nurtured, and energized.

The Flow of Energy

What is Qi?

In its earliest contexts, Qi (pronounced "Chi") was a meteorological category composed of six phases – cold, warmth, wind, rain, darkness, and light. Qi originally referred to steam or vapor, but by the time of Confucius, it indicated an animating force in the atmosphere, manifested in weather. This force was thought to actively influence the human body, showing itself in chills, fever, delusions, and sickness. The science of Feng Shui analyzed this force in the environment with the intention of controlling its manifestations in the individual. Later, when other factors such as numerology and astrology were added to the mix, Feng Shui became less a science and more an art.

Heaven Qi	Earth Qi	Human Qi
Planetary Qi	**Natural Qi:**	**Social Qi:**
Universal Qi	Vegetation	Political and Cultural
Astrology	Landforms	Social Contacts
Sun, Moon, and Planets	Mountains	Neighbors
Cycles of Change	Valleys and Plains	Partner, Family, or Relatives
Spiritual Guidance	Rivers and the Sea	Local Events, Community
	Magnetic Fields	
Weather Qi	Earth and Energies	**Personal Qi:**
Sunlight	Latitude and Longitude	Memories and Visions
Clouds and Rain		Ideals and Beliefs
Wind	**Human-made Qi:**	Personality and Integrity
Seasons	External Built Environments	Sensitivity
Tide	Internal Environments	Health and Life-force
Heat and Cold	Interior Design, Layout, and Proportions	
	Color, Light, and Sound	

The Book of Burial characterizes Qi as "life breath." While this ancient text is an accurate description, Qi is much more significant than this phrase indicates. Qi is energy. It is the driving life-force and moral fiber of human beings. A person of great will or charisma has strong Qi. It is the sign of artful skill, in writing, painting, calligraphy. Or, if a person is unwell, his Qi is considered weak. The Taoists claim that each person possesses three treasures: Jing – hormones, blood and other biochemical components of the body; Qi – breath, energy and life-force; and Shen – intellect and spirit.

But Qi does not only flow through our bodies; it flows through our cosmos and our Earth. It is the invisible force of all animate things, the quality of environments, the power of the sun, the moon and weather systems.

The purpose of Feng Shui is to create environments in which Qi flows smoothly. Where beneficial Qi (Sheng Qi) meanders gently along curved lines through the interiors of a home, the occupants will feel positive, nurtured, energized. The occupants of a home filled with negative Qi (Shar Qi) will find the environment oppressive, stagnant, stale. Unlike Sheng Qi, Shar Qi strikes quickly, in straight lines; if Qi flows too quickly, a strong, forceful energy called a "poison arrow" is created, producing a feeling of disharmony where it hits the house or room.

Poison arrows can be created by sharp angles from neighboring buildings and telephone poles, by other straight lines, such as roads or driveways leading to your front door, or by long corridors in the house. The flow of Qi is also affected by the shape of the house, the shape of the block of land and the environment around it.

Opposite below: The aim of Feng Shui is to maintain harmony and balance between heaven, earth and human Qi. In heaven, there is tien Qi (tian chi) or heaven Qi; on earth there is di Qi (te chi) or earth Qi; and within each of us there is ren Qi (ren chi) or human Qi. Heaven Qi is comprised of forces which heavenly bodies exert on Earth such as heat, rain, and drought. Earth Qi is affected by heaven Qi – too much rain causes flooding, too little will cause plants to die. Within the earth Qi, each person has his or her own individual Qi.

Below: Qi not only flows through our bodies; it flows through our cosmos and our Earth as well. It is the invisible force of all animate things, the quality of environments, the power of the sun, the moon and weather systems.

Above: A yin room, home or environment, is cool, passive and calming – such as this sideboard in an inner-city entrance. Colors in the yin category tend to be organic and fertile greens; soft, dreamy blues or pale violets. Organic, rounded, introverted, quiet rooms tend to be yin. Soft furnishings, fluffy rugs, throw rugs and wall tapestries are all yin.

Below: In interior design terms, a room decorated in hot, positive colors such as bright red, hot pink, orange or vibrant yellow is yang. Yang rooms such as the living room, home office or kitchen are filled with energy, movement and discussion. Striking features or objects, such as metal sculptures, bright paint, lights, mirrors, ceramics and hardwood floors are yang; so are sharp angles and sunlight.

Yin and Yang

The oldest anthology of poetry in Chinese tradition, *The Book of Odes*, recounts the tale of Chief Gong Liu, who bravely led an exodus of his people to the fertile lands of Bin in the year 1796 BCE. Upon arrival in his new domain, Chief Liu conducted a geophysical survey. He measured the shadow of the sundial to determine the cardinal directions. According to tradition, "sunshine and shade," as depicted in the poem, are the original forerunners for the terms "yin" and "yang."

In a nutshell, yin and yang represent all the opposing yet interdependent energies of the universe. The tai chi, the symbol for yin and yang, provides a visual explanation. Comprised of half circles (but not semicircles) – one dark, the other light – each is at its greatest where the other begins, and as each diminishes the other grows. Within the dark half is a seed of light and within the light half is a seed of dark. Each gives rise and meaning to the other.

Yin (negative) and yang (positive) are forces, in constant movement, acting together to create energy. Just as night would not exist without day, we cannot have dark without light, nor shadow without sun. An underlying concept of Feng Shui is how to achieve balance between these two opposing forces within our own lives and environments.

In short, yang conveys everything overt, bright, active, masculine; yin is the more secretive, dark, passive, feminine state. In interior design terms, a room decorated in hot, positive yang colors would be bright red, hot pink, orange or vibrant yellow. Rooms such as the living or entertaining spaces of the home, which contain striking features such as metal sculptures, bright paintwork and bold feature walls, tend to be yang. Insertions such as mirrors, stone bowls, ceramics, hardwood floors and concrete are yang; as are ventilated, sunlit, sharply angled rooms.

A yin room, on the other hand, such as a bathroom or bedroom, is cool and passive. Colors in this category are soft, dreamy blues and greens. Organic, rounded, introverted, quiet rooms tend to be yin. Soft furnishings, fluffy rugs, throw rugs and wall tapestries are all yin. Each has the ability to affect moods, or the "feeling" you have when you step into a room – exhilarated, relaxed, energized or subdued.

In the home, yang must be the dominant energy. Too much yin energy can be gloomy and oppressive. On the other hand, overpowering yang will lead to sleeplessness and an inability to concentrate and function efficiently. Where either yin or yang achieves dominance, an imbalance occurs. The balance of yin and yang encourages the effective, positive flow of Qi. It is this positive flow of Qi which is manipulated by effective Feng Shui, by correct interior design, which is itself facilitated by an understanding of yin and yang.

The trick to energizing a yin area is to charge it with a yang spot. Or, to decrease an overexuberant yang area, ground it with some soft yin tones. If you have a hardwood timber or tile floor (yang), add the cozy warmth of a rug (yin) to balance it. If there's too much yang energy in the living room, cover the couch with soft cushions in gentle colors. Put up a wall hanging. Equally, if you have a dark yin room, the addition of bright flowers or an aquarium will provide it with much-needed yang energy.

Page 17: While too much yin energy can be gloomy and oppressive, too much yang energy, such as the glaring sunlight and stark whiteness of this room, should be balanced with much-needed yin features such as soft green plants, art work or soft furnishings to help ground the energy.

Above: This contemporary bedroom was too yang for rest, relaxation and romance, so the vibrant energy of the orange tones and hues was diffused by the application of soft, earthy yin coverings and cushions. Yang colors (especially bright orange) aren't good Feng Shui in the bedroom unless balanced sensitively with yin colors or shapes.

Above: The trick to energizing a yin area is to charge it with a yang spot. This dark yin room was enlivened with much-needed yang energy by the use of burning candles, and a lighter bedspread and throw blanket. The window was also opened and curtains were tied back, to allow for ventilation and sunlight.

Above: The cozy warmth of a rug (yin) was applied to this concrete floor (yang), to balance the opposing elements. Apply this concept if you have a hardwood timber, tile or concrete floor; sparse walls benefit from a wall hanging, tapestry or painting.

Yin and yang

	Yin	Yang
Concept	Dark	Bright
	Cold	Hot
	Heavy	Light
	Wet	Dry
	Soft	Hard
Aspect	Feminine	Masculine
	Stillness	Movement
	Passive	Active
	Sleep	Wakefulness
Representation	Moon	Sun
	Winter	Summer
	Valley	Mountain
	Earth	Heaven
Directions	Below	Above
	Down	Up
	Right	Left
	Back	Front
	In	Out
Numbers	Odd Numbers	Even Numbers
Colors	Blues/Greens	Warm Red Tones
Architecture	Interior	Exterior
	Empty Space	Solid Structure
	Gardens	Houses
	Curved	Geometric

Above: Yin (negative) and yang (positive) are representative of all the opposite energies or forces of the universe. In constant movement, yin and yang act together to create energy. The symbol for yin and yang, the tai chi, makes it easy for us to understand. Comprising two halves joined together – one part dark, the other light – each gives rise and meaning to the other. Each is at its greatest where the other begins, and as each diminishes the other grows. Within the dark section is a speck of light, and within the light section is a speck of dark.

The Chinese System of Elements

The Chinese recognize five elements. These arise out of the interplay of yin and yang and represent different manifestations of Qi. They represent a classification system for everything in the universe, including people. The Chinese believe everything is in a constant state of change, moving among the five elements or forces of nature – these are called wu-xing (woo-shing).

These five elements are another key to manipulating Qi in the home. They are Water or Shui (Shwee), Wood or Mu (Moo), Fire or Huo (Hor), Earth or T'u (Too), Metal or Jin (Chin). The Chinese elements are thought of as changing energies, each with five different sets of qualities.

Below, left to right: The five elements – Water, Wood, Fire, Earth, Metal – are represented by symbolic association in the home and are a key Feng Shui principle used for manipulating Qi. The Fire element in the home is symbolized by candles, lights and lamps. Aquariums, ponds, water features symbolize Water. Bricks and terracotta symbolize the Earth element. Wooden furniture and decking are symbolic of Wood. Kitchenware, clocks and plates symbolize Metal.

Ideally, there should be a balance of all the elements. Where one dominates or is lacking, difficulties occur. Interpreting and balancing the elements plays a major role in the practice of Feng Shui. They also constitute an easy way of identifying the correct elements of a Feng Shui makeover, where the most important associations are, and how the five elements relate to the eight compass directions.

The production/destruction cycle

The elements move and relate to each other in a productive/destructive manner. This forms a cycle, which can be productive and creative, or potentially destructive and negative. Consider the cycle in the following manner: Water enables Wood to grow, Wood enables Fire to burn, resulting in ashes on Earth, in which forms Metal, which in liquid form resembles Water. Or another cycle: Water extinguishes Fire, and in turn is soaked up by the Earth, which is depleted of energy by Wood in the form of trees, which can be destroyed by Metal tools. We must also remember that in supporting another element, an element can itself be weakened.

Above: By understanding how each energy is represented in your home, you can easily change the feel of your environment. For example, once you know that Fire energy is active and energizing, you can apply its symbols where appropriate – a glowing fireplace in the living room or a candlelit dinner for two will promote good Feng Shui.

Above: The Bagua, or Pa Kua is perhaps the most important reference symbol in the practice of Feng Shui. This octagonal symbol corresponds to the four cardinal points of the compass and its four sub-directions. The four cardinal compass points are North (N), South (S), East (E) and West (W). Between them are inter-cardinal points: Northwest (NW), Northeast (NE), Southwest (SW) and Southeast (SE). Each direction corresponds to one of the eight trigrams of Chinese metaphysics, derived from the ancient text the *I Ching*.

Fire

SYMBOLIZES: Fire, heat, summer.

DIRECTION: South.

POSITIVES: Warmth, happiness, light. Positive Fire characteristics include innovation, passion, action and humor.

NEGATIVES: Fire can erupt, explode and destroy. It can evoke impatience, anger or inconsiderate actions.

ASSOCIATIONS: Symbols of the sun. Candles, lights and lamps. All manufactured materials. Triangular or pyramid shapes. Geometric patterns. Warm red tones. Plants with pointed leaves. A skylight or fireplace.

THE PRODUCTION/DESTRUCTION CYCLE: Fire is helped by Wood, harmed by Water, weakened by Earth. Fire weakens Metal.

Wood

SYMBOLIZES: Growth, renewal, plant life. Wood energy is nurturing, versatile and expansive.

DIRECTION: East/Southeast.

POSITIVES: It can be as supple and pliable as bamboo or as sturdy as oak. Positive Wood characteristics include visualization, artistic talent, enthusiasm, public-mindedness.

NEGATIVES: Wood can be used as a spear. Negative Wood characteristics include impatience, anger, an inability to complete tasks.

ASSOCIATIONS: Trees, plants, flowers. Wooden furniture or decorative objects made from wood. Paper, columns, decking. The color green. Artwork depicting landscapes. Tall plants, vertically striped blinds or uplights.

THE PRODUCTION/DESTRUCTION CYCLE: Wood is helped by Water, harmed by Metal, weakened by Fire. Wood weakens Earth.

Earth

SYMBOLIZES: Nurturing environment which enables seeds to grow. Earth supports, nurtures and interacts with each of the other elements.

DIRECTION: Center/Southwest/Northeast.

POSITIVES: Earth denotes fairness, wisdom, instinct. Positive Earth characteristics include loyalty, patience and practicality.

NEGATIVES: Earth can smother. Negative Earth characteristics include obsession and nit-picking.

ASSOCIATIONS: Clay, brick, terracotta. Ochre. Cement and stone. Squares. Yellow, brown, orange. Ceramic bowls, porcelain jars, pots, furnishings in earth tones. Low, wide, and cube-shaped objects such as coffee tables or ottomans. Low, spreading plants.

THE PRODUCTION/DESTRUCTION CYCLE: Earth is helped by Fire, harmed by Wood, weakened by Metal. Earth weakens Water.

Metal

SYMBOLIZES: Autumn. Strength. It represents solidity and an ability to "contain" objects. Metal is also a conductor.

DIRECTION: West/Northwest.

POSITIVES: Communication, brilliant ideas, justice. Positive Metal characteristics include independence and intuition.

NEGATIVES: Destruction, danger, sadness. Can be the blade of a weapon. Can evoke inflexibility, seriousness, melancholy.

ASSOCIATIONS: All metals. Metal objects. Kitchenware. Coins. Clocks. The colors white, gray, silver and gold. Domes. Round shapes. Candlesticks, plates, photo frames, polished hard stone surfaces, including marble or granite.

THE PRODUCTION/DESTRUCTION CYCLE: Metal is helped by Earth, harmed by Fire, weakened by Water. Metal weakens Wood.

Water

SYMBOLIZES: Winter and water. The inner self, art, beauty.

DIRECTION: North.

POSITIVES: It nurtures and supports with understanding. Positive Water characteristics include diplomacy, sociability, sympathy, artistry.

NEGATIVES: Water can wear down and exhaust. It can suggest fear, nervousness, and stress. Negative Water characteristics include oversensitivity and fickleness.

ASSOCIATIONS: Rivers, streams, lakes. Water features. Reflective materials, including mirrors and glass. Fish tanks. Artwork depicting water. The colors blue and black. A decorative blue lantern or sculpture, blue sofa, black shelving, a textured glass bowl, creeping plants.

THE PRODUCTION/DESTRUCTION CYCLE: Water is helped by Metal, harmed by Earth, weakened by Wood. Water weakens Fire.

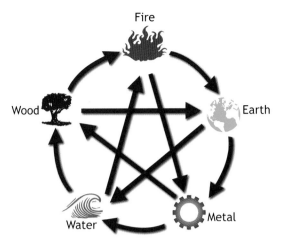

Above: The Elements move in a predetermined way, in a cycle where they all support each other. Consider the cycle in the following manner: Water enables Wood to grow, Wood enables Fire to burn, resulting in ashes on Earth, in which forms Metal, which in liquid form resembles Water. It is important to remember that in supporting another element, an element itself can be weakened.

Wood

Fire   Water

Metal   Earth

Art Meets Science
Feng Shui Tools

The Bagua

The principal reference symbol in the practice of Feng Shui is the Bagua, or Pa Kua. This octagonal symbol corresponds to the four cardinal points of the compass and their four sub-directions. The four cardinal compass points are North (N), South (S), East (E) and West (W). Halfway between them are inter-cardinal points: Northwest (NW), Northeast (NE), Southwest (SW) and Southeast (SE). Each direction corresponds to one of the eight trigrams of Chinese metaphysics, derived from the *I Ching*. Trigrams are representative of our journey through life – each trigram has its own multiple sets of meanings, as well as supplementary symbols and connotations.

Each side of the Bagua also represents a life aspiration. The life aspiration areas are: mentors and networking, romance and marriage, family and ancestors, wealth and prosperity, career, recognition and fame, education and knowledge and, finally, children. These life aspirations are discussed more fully in later chapters.

In a nutshell, the basis of Feng Shui is about identifying your particular problem areas (or where you're currently "stuck") in relation to these life aspirations and how they have manifested physically in your home and living environment. Problem areas can manifest themselves as clutter, stagnant or unbalanced corners, neglected or unusually shaped rooms and inappropriately placed storage such as under a bed or over a work area. Identifying problem areas can be achieved by placing the Bagua over a plan of your home or room; enabling you to rectify and balance trouble spots and allow for more free-flowing energy in your life and home.

The symbols and directions of the Bagua are used as guides to create comfortable living and working environments. It is an ancient Chinese

Opposite: Although tools such as the Bagua, the Lo Shu or Magic Square assist with the practice of Feng Shui, everyday objects play their own role in its implementation. Bowls of brightly colored objects, lamps, artefacts and furniture all serve to direct or concentrate energy in the home.

Below: This Bagua shows the various attributes which have been attached to the eight main directions by different Feng Shui systems. All the symbols belonging to one side of the Bagua are believed to be in harmony, complementary to each other. To create comfortable or auspicious living and working environments, the symbols and directions of the Bagua are used as guides by Feng Shui masters.

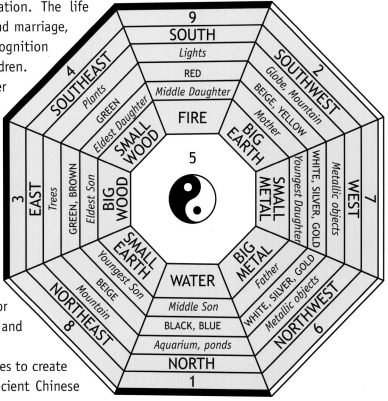

principle that applying positive Feng Shui to specific corners or sectors of the home encourages beneficial manifestations such as harmony, luck and fortune in your life. For example, you can activate the relationships corner of your home or bedroom if you are looking for a partner, or place symbols of prosperity in the wealth sector of your home office.

To apply the Bagua effectively, you will need a plan of your house drawn to scale – graph paper makes it easier – and you will need to find the center and the front of your home. Then you will need a compass to align the Bagua with the relevant directions that each room faces. The front door is regarded as the "mouth" of the home, because it is where energy comes into your home. Paradoxically, the "mouth" doesn't have to be a dedicated front door, just the door you and your loved ones use regularly to enter the home. Regardless of where your front door is, it will always

Above: A Feng Shui tape, known as a Luben ruler, is just one of the tools you can use for measuring and dividing rooms in the home. Unlike the layman's measuring tape, used purely for the purposes of measuring, a Feng Shui tape also contains a repeated sequence of eight characters, representing auspicious and inauspicious categories. The eight characters symbolize: Ben (origin), Hai (harmful), Tie (robbery), Guan (official), Yi (righteousness), Li (separation), Blng (sickness) and Cai (wealth).

Right: To apply the Bagua effectively, you will need a plan of your house drawn to scale – graph paper makes it easier – and you will need to find the center and the front of your home. Then you will need a compass to align the Bagua with the directions each room faces. By superimposing the Bagua over the plan of your entire home, or just one room, you can identify the problems associated with unusual, unbalanced shapes. Missing corners could indicate particular difficulties. If it's the relationships corner, it could indicate a growing rift in a marriage or partnership; if it's the fame/acknowledgment corner, perhaps your attempts at acknowledgment in a project are proving futile. In this house, the front entrance is in the knowledge area. Part of the fame/acknowledgment and relationship areas are missing and will need the application of Feng Shui remedies.

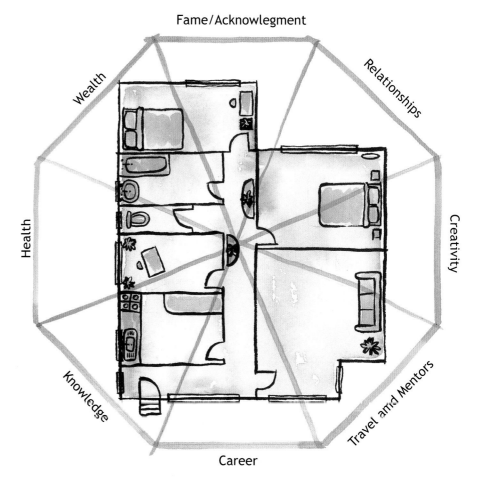

Fame/Acknowlegment

Wealth

Relationships

Health

Creativity

Knowledge

Travel and Mentors

Career

fall in one of these three areas, center (career), to the right of the center as you are facing it (travel and mentors) or to the left (knowledge and intuition).

By superimposing the Bagua over your plan of your entire home or just one room you can identify the problems associated with unusual, unbalanced shapes. Missing corners could indicate particular difficulties. If it's the career corner, it could mean difficulties at work; if it's the health corner it could be an ongoing illness. Going through your home room by room will help you understand where energy is stagnant or stale and where it needs to be cured by the application of Feng Shui.

The Lo Shu Magic Square

The good news is that the vast amount of information associated with the compass directions has been reduced to a shorthand form incorporated in the Magic Square. Many formulas based on the magic square are used to establish whether or not a place is auspicious. The Magic Square became the foundation of Taoist practice, and many of Taoism's rituals continue to be synchronized with its pattern.

According to history books of old China, the Magic Square dates back to 2005 BCE. The magic square is arranged so that when three numbers are added together, whether they are in a horizontal, vertical or diagonal line, the result is always 15, which also happens to be the number of days it takes for the new moon to become a full moon. The square has exerted a powerful influence on Chinese cultural symbolism, and the pattern of numbers has become inextricably linked with the trigrams of the Bagua. At the same time, the symbolism of the grid was extended to create connections between the numbers and the four celestial animals – the dragon, the tiger, the turtle and the phoenix. These animals are symbolic of the landscape or cityscape which surrounds a home, building or city. The phoenix is the distant front view; the turtle is the protective hill (or building) at the back; the dragon is to the left and the tiger is to the right. When a home is considered auspicious, all four symbolic animals surround it in a protective manner.

Correlations between the Magic Square and the Bagua become apparent when the grid is superimposed onto the Bagua using the compass directions as a guide – south is always equated with the number nine, and north is always represented by the number one. With the numbers in place, the Magic Square then unlocks further meanings within the Bagua.

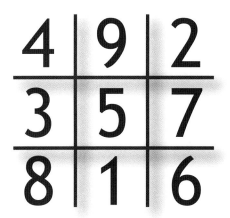

Above: The "magic" in the Chinese Magic Square lies in the fact that every line of three numbers, whether chosen in a horizontal, vertical or diagonal line, always adds up to the number 15, which is also the number of days it takes for the new moon to become a full moon. This particular pattern of numbers is also linked with the trigrams and symbolism of the Bagua.

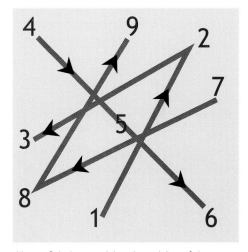

Above: Scholars studying the origins of the Magic Square have speculated on the remarkable similarities between the grid's numbers and the ancient Hebrew sign for the planet Saturn. Dating back to 2005 BCE, the Magic Square became the foundation of Taoist magical practice. And today, many of Taoism's magic rituals continue to be synchronized in accordance with its "magical" pattern.

Life Aspirations and Sacred Spaces

Once deciding which life aspiration you wish to enhance or "activate," there is a variety of tools you can use. The style of decorative objects isn't important – that's up to you. What is important is that items – whether a photograph, a splash of color, natural crystals or river pebbles – are consciously selected and placed. In every moment in every space, create an expression of beauty, reflection and thoughtfulness. First, though, you need to define and be clear about your own objectives. Ask yourself some questions. What's happening in your relationships? Have you found your path in life? Then activate the areas where you feel a need for change.

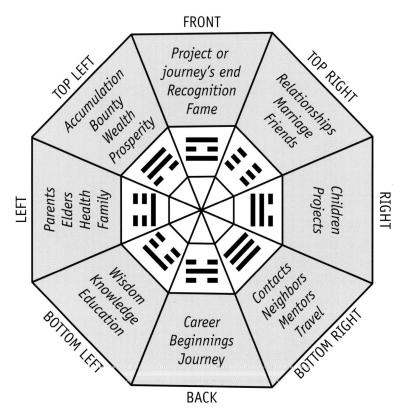

CAREER/KNOWLEDGE: Relates to our journey, path or purpose in life – either in our jobs or our personal experiences and growth. It also depicts the commencement of a project or assignment, a career change or a new job.

BAGUA ASSOCIATIONS: Water, black, second son, ear.

ACTIVATING SACRED SPACE: Installing a fishbowl in this sector of your home or room will activate your career, but avoid going overboard and introducing a very large tank – too much water can drown your prospects. Goldfish are good Feng Shui, but avoid predatory fish. A water feature in constant movement is a good option. In this sector, hang images depicting energy and movement. Pin up images of an aspiration – great poets you admire if you're a writer, a theater where you'd like to perform, or a university where you wish to study. Place books, framed words of wisdom and pictures of mentors in the area. Hang crystals in the window, or apply glass objects to increase the energy and positive Qi flow.

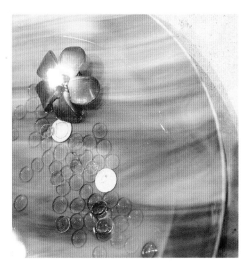

Above: Here is a feature which represents all five elements, will act as an enhancer for any space and will nurture the supportive energy in your home. Fill a glass or crystal bowl (Earth) with blue glass nuggets (Earth and Water), then fill with water and floating candles (Fire) and some flowers or petals (Wood). Add coins (Metal) to complete the cycle.

RELATIONSHIPS: Relates to associating well with people and having the support of partners, family and friends. Also marriage prospects, romance, partnerships.

BAGUA ASSOCIATIONS: Earth, pink/peach, mother, organs.

ACTIVATING SACRED SPACE: Try double images for romance – two vases, two candlesticks, a photograph of yourself with your loved one or a group of friends. Double images are positive Feng Shui, while single images depict loneliness. Display a collection of objects in pink, peach, red. Natural crystals, particularly if combined with the light of a chandelier, will activate this sector, as will images of cherubs, angels or spiritual figures. Plants, ribbons or wind-activated objects (only if there is a breeze – if there's no breeze, don't use them) all help improve the flow of Qi.

FAMILY/ANCESTORS: Relates to clan, heritage, parents. Our families, past and present, color who we are, how we relate to the world and interact with others. How are you presently interacting with your family?

BAGUA ASSOCIATIONS: Thunder, wood, pale green, first son, foot.

ACTIVATING SACRED SPACE: Apply family photographs, documents, heirlooms and antiques. Placing plants and flowers in this sector enhances family relationships, while activating positive Qi. But make sure they are healthy – discard any which are dried or dead. Choose plants with broad, healthy leaves, and avoid cacti. A small aquarium is good in this sector, but make sure it is kept clean. Use green colors in furnishings.

MENTORS/NETWORKING: Relates to clients, charity, travel and interaction with others. Religious or spiritual advisers are also depicted here. If you are willing to help others and need some help in return, this is the area to focus on.

BAGUA ASSOCIATIONS: Heaven, metal, white, father, head.

ACTIVATING SACRED SPACE: Create altars, use incense. Place musical instruments, either real or decorative – such as bells, guitars, drums – in this area, and melodious metal wind chimes, especially if there's a breeze. Use metal objects and inspirational quotes and pictures. Also, store your telephone, telephone directories or business cards in this sector.

WEALTH/PROSPERITY: Often taken to mean monetary wealth, but also relates to the richness and abundance of our lives, fulfillment and the accumulation of beneficial energies around us.

BAGUA ASSOCIATIONS: Wind, wood, dark green/purple, eldest daughter, hip.

ACTIVATING SACRED SPACE: Hang six or eight *I Ching* coins in this sector to create auspicious Feng Shui; alternatively, use other decorative coins. Place empty bowls around and remove clutter. Images depicting movement, or an indoor water feature (such as a small aquarium), are also good in this sector. In bathrooms, always keep the toilet lid down and drains covered; otherwise, your wealth could drain away.

FAME/ACKNOWLEDGMENT: Relates to fame, recognition, status. Not notoriety for its own sake, but recognition of an undertaking well done and a sense of fulfillment. What do you need to do to gain recognition for what you do?

BAGUA ASSOCIATIONS: Fire red, maroon/mauve, second daughter, eye.

ACTIVATING SACRED SPACE: Install a bright light – the brighter the better. Bright lights are wonderful conductors of good Feng Shui. Also, use red objects, mobiles, burning candles, candelabras, chandeliers or oil burners. Place images of the sun or fire in the area. Having your fireplace, stove or heaters in this sector is extremely beneficial. Also, try pinning up certificates, newspaper cuttings or other products of your achievement.

CENTER: Tai Chi, health.

BAGUA ASSOCIATIONS: Earth, yellow, center.

ACTIVATING SACRED SPACE: The center of the home or room is an excellent spot for an interior courtyard garden. If this is not possible, try applying a round rug, a round table or hanging a chandelier. It is best to avoid locating the bathroom in this sector. Ensure that the center of the home is kept clean and open.

Below far left: Placing flowers or plants in the family/ancestors sector of a house or room will activate family relationships, affecting how we interact with others. Make sure the plants you choose are healthy – discard any which are dried or dead. Select plants with broad leaves, not pointed ones, and avoid spiky plants and cacti.

Below second from left: The fame/acknowledgment sector of this home office has been activated with positive, powerful Feng Shui conductors: a fiery maroon dragon and bright burning candles. Other beneficial sacred space enhancers for this sector include chandeliers, oil burners, certificates of achievement or newspaper cuttings which relate to your quest for fame or acknowledgment.

Below second from right: Applying crystals or glass objects will increase the energy and positive flow of Qi in the career/knowledge sector of a house or room. The career/knowledge sector relates to our journey, path and purpose in life – either in our jobs or related to our personal experiences and personal growth.

Below far right: Here an empty bowl has been used to activate the sacred space in the wealth/prosperity corner of a living room. Often interpreted as relating only to monetary wealth, this sector actually also relates to the richness, abundance and fulfilment of our lives, and to the accumulation of beneficial energies around us.

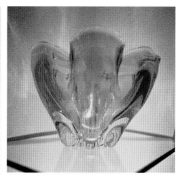

Numbers and Directions

Kua number	Best direction	Elements
1	SE, E, S, N	Water
2	NE, W, NW, SW	Earth
3	S, N, SE, E	Wood
4	N, S, E, SE	Wood
5 (Male)	NE, W, NW, SW	Earth
5 (Female)	SW, NW, W, NE	Earth
6	W, NE, SW, NW	Metal
7	NW, SW, NE, W	Metal
8	SW, NW, W, NE	Earth
9	E, SE, N, S	Fire

According to ancient Chinese principles, it's desirable that the orientation of your home, or of the room in which you spend the greatest amount of time, faces your best direction. It is believed that facing your best direction will support the activities you perform in that space. For example, those who fall into the east category should face their houses toward the east; west category people should face toward the west. The position of your work desk, and where you sleep should also follow these principles – unfortunately, this is not always possible.

Auspicious and inauspicious locations differ from person to person. To identify the four auspicious locations which will bring you different kinds of good fortune, you first need to calculate your Kua number. There are two different kinds of formulas for working out your Kua number – one for males, the other for females. Some Feng Shui consultants only use the male, or yang, numbers in their calculations; some use both male and female, or yin, numbers. Others regard the yin as a representation of the inner self and the yang as the image a person presents to the world.

Calculating your Kua number

KUA NUMBER FOR MALES
Take the year of your birth and add together the last two digits. (If the result is 10 or more, add the two digits to reduce them to a single number.) Deduct the result from 10 – the result is your Kua number.

Year of Birth = 1954
Add last two numbers = 5+4
Total = 9
Male deducts total from ten = 10-9
Kua number of males born in 1954 = 1

KUA NUMBER FOR FEMALES
Take the year of your birth and add together the last two digits. (If the result is 10 or more, add the two digits to reduce them to a single number.) Then add five – the answer is your Kua number. (If this second result is 10 or more, add the two digits to reduce them to a single number – the answer is your Kua number.)

Year of Birth = 1960
Add last two numbers = 6+0
Total = 6
Females add 5 to total – 6+5
If the new number is two digits, add these together = 11
Total = 1+1
Kua number of females born in 1960 = 2

Above: Rooflines can be symbolically compared to hill shapes, and to their elemental associations. This gentle, shallow roof pitch is ideal, as it represents a gentle, undulating mountain.

Above: Steeply pitched roofs represent the Fire element, and are considered to be inauspicious. If you are in the fortunate position of designing or selecting your home, make roof pitch and balance a high priority. Also, keep an eye on the dimensions of the house relative to its surrounding environment – because the trees surrounding this house are tall, the pitched roof isn't out of proportion. Applying good Feng Shui is about creating and maintaining balance between the various elements of your environment.

Home as Sanctuary

Design, Site, and Shape

Introduction

The practice of site selection was first recorded in the middle of the Shang Dynasty (1755–1046 BCE), when royal diviners queried Shang Di, the High God, on the efficacy of a particular time for establishing a city. These particular ancient textual passages were recorded on oracle bones; from this time, it is thought that this method of divination was also used to determine the efficacy of a particular place.

Whether you live in an urban environment or in a country location, there are elements to consider when selecting and assessing a site. If you're about to move, or are fortunate enough to have a site, choices you make have the capacity to affect your well-being and happiness. Investigating the immediate environment is a good start. Issues might include proximity to schools, parks, the town center or your workplace, plus proposed road and building developments or local architecture. Natural phenomena must also be taken into consideration. Rainfall, flood areas, wind direction, sun direction, soil type, height above sea level and geological faults are also relevant.

You need to remember that the modern world has problems which did not exist in the ancient world, and these must be taken into consideration when applying Feng Shui today. In the ancient world, auspicious site selection wasn't hampered by the negative aspects of factories, gas stations, electricity sub-stations, skyscrapers, 24-hour nightclubs, traffic or airports. Over a period of time, the by-products of modern living have the capacity to affect our general health, physiological well-being and ability to relax. This is particularly the case if these elements are in close proximity to, or have an affect on, the noise or pollution levels around your home. The art and science of Feng Shui can help us identify these influences and guide us with precautionary measures.

The illustrations below represent various inauspicious house shapes. Square or rectangular houses are much more conducive to good Feng Shui than those which have protruding extensions, or which are L-shaped, U-shaped or wedge-shaped. Avoid houses with too many corners or sharp angles.

Above: An L-shaped house is considered inauspicious – the Chinese believe an L-shaped house resembles a knife or meat cleaver. This shape will bring bad fortune to its residents.

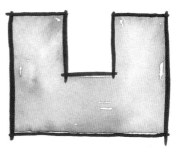

Above: The residents of a U-shaped house face equally bad fortune. This configuration is thought to bring unhappiness.

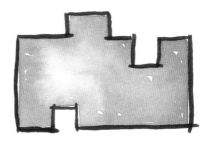

Above: This illustration shows a house with too many sharp angles and corners – these can create hard-hitting poison arrows.

House design and balance

Good Feng Shui is about creating and maintaining balance between the various elements of the environment. When designing or selecting your home, keep balance as a high priority. Keep an eye on the dimensions of the house relative to its surrounding environment. Look at the size and number of the doors, windows and rooms. Balance sun-filled and shaded areas within the home, greenery and bricked areas, colors, the elements of yin and yang and the five elements.

Interior balance is also reflected in the ratio of windows to doors and in the size and height of the rooms. Large, airy rooms are better than small rooms, but they should not be too large, too high or out of proportion with the home. The direction a building faces will affect its Qi – when a building doesn't receive any sun for light, warmth and color, the energy inside it can become stagnant and stale. A house flooded with sunshine, on the other hand, will have strong yang energy, and will need to be cooled with softer yin colors.

Balance creates harmony, which in turn creates good Qi in the home. If your home is so large that it dominates your site, ensure that you have compensating features designed into the house plan – outdoor lights can extend the yard, and dark color schemes can balance the yang force of such a house. Plots with generous amounts of land, on the other hand, are excellent, and conducive to the flow of Qi. Miserly and constrained dwellings stifle the flow of Qi.

A house in the center of the plot, with neither the front nor the back yard too spacious or too constrained, is best. Trees or plants are an excellent way to camouflage irregularities. If you are in doubt about which way to position your house, look for land which allows you to face south. Many Feng Shui masters in both the southern and northern hemispheres advocate this, based on the belief that the south is a source of wealth. Some Feng Shui practitioners maintain that where terrain has been scarred or cut, the exposed earth symbolizes the blood of an injured dragon. Others claim the worst direction for your home is facing northeast, as it represents the 'gateway of hell.' Whatever the direction your home faces, it is important to ensure the front is not messy or overgrown, making it hard to access.

Good design and balance are not isolated to the structure and direction of your home, they also relate to your plot of land. It is considered vital for tapping auspicious 'earth luck' to maintain a balanced relationship between the two.

House shapes

Square or rectangular shapes are much more conducive to Feng Shui than those which have protruding extensions, or which are L-shaped, U-shaped or wedge-shaped. Regularly shaped houses are considered balanced and complete, lending themselves to Feng Shui enhancement.

Houses with too many corners are to be avoided. The sharp angles are bad Feng Shui. The Chinese believe that L-shaped houses create imbalance, and so bring bad fortune – they should be avoided at all costs.

The residents of a U-shaped house face equally bad fortune. The rules for house shapes also apply to apartment shapes. Square or rectangular layouts are preferable. As this is seldom possible, it is advisable to try to do something about correcting an irregular shape. Mirrors can be used to extend L-shaped apartments. A bank of lights can be placed along the wall of an elongated apartment to extend its shape.

Try to avoid large or many-angled roof lines, as these cause harm to neighboring properties. In symbolic terms, roof lines can be compared to hill shapes, and to their elemental associations. It is advisable to check the productive and destructive cycles of the elements. Roofs which have a shallow pitch resemble hills, which are linked to the Earth element, and are auspicious. Steeply pitched roofs represent the Fire element and are inauspicious. Apartment blocks with flat roofs suggest hills with flat plateaus – these are not very favorable. The ideal is to have a gentle, sloping roof line, which represents gentle, undulating mountain shapes.

Above: A square house or apartment is considered very auspicious, bringing good luck to the residents.

Above: A rectangular dwelling, as shown here, is preferable to an irregularly shaped one.

The same rules apply to apartment shapes as to house shapes. Regularly shaped dwellings, such as square or rectangular layouts, are considered balanced and complete, lending themselves to positive Feng Shui. Unfortunately, apartments with these shapes are rare; it is advisable to try to do something to correct irregularly shaped apartments. Mirrors can be used to extend L-shaped apartments. Or a bank of lights can be placed along the long wall of an elongated apartment to extend its shape.

Urban Living

Striking a balance when living in an urban environment is important, but often difficult. Whether your choice to live in the city is work or lifestyle related, there are many elements to consider. Often, urban life seems to "run away" on you – working weeks roll around quickly, it's noisy, there's traffic, it's polluted and overpopulated. Some people thrive on what it has to offer – the galleries, great shopping, dining out, going to the theater. Whatever your view, having a quiet, safe, and private sanctuary to come home to can make all the difference.

Many urban homes are boxed-in apartments with no outlook, aspect or garden. To decrease the yang energy found here and in the center of large cities, interior colorings should be yin. Opt for muted tones, natural floorings, plants, soft furnishings. If the town center is small, its feeling can be yin – it's lonely and mysterious when it closes down at night. In this instance, home interiors should be cheerfully yang – select bright tones, colorful rugs, ottomans, artwork and flowers. The suburbs may also be mainly yin, if there is little night activity, so balance your suburban home with yang tones and objects.

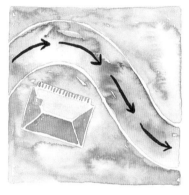

Above: Qi travels quickly along straight urban roads – this affects houses or buildings at the end of long T-junctions or busy intersections. This phenomenon also helps explain why businesses in this position are often difficult to lease or sell.

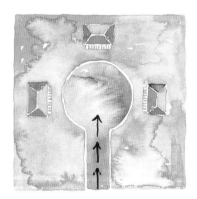

Above: The best location for a home is where Qi meanders, in the inner bend of a river or road.

Above: The residents in this cul-de-sac will find Qi hard hitting – they are likely to feel agitated and unable to relax.

Right: This terrace house in the heart of the city is a private sanctuary from the outside world, with sensitively designed interiors, muted tones, lighting, plants and soft furnishings throughout. In the center of large cities, yang energy is abundant, so interior colorings and applications should ideally be yin, to balance the excessive yang energy. The opposite applies to outer suburbs (yin), which need to be brought to life with vibrant (yang) interiors.

Rooms in warehouse spaces tend to stretch on forever, with their high ceilings, massive windows, and lack of dividing walls. Here it's often difficult to ground the energy, so introduce plants and cozy, comfortable yin areas – use screens, curtains, cushions or color to create boundaries between spaces. An easy way to achieve this is to create "small spaces" within a large area. Selectively cluster furniture together according to the various functions for living. Spaces for relaxing might include comfortable soft furnishings such as couches, armchairs, cushions or rugs. A work or study space might be defined by a length of fabric hanging from the ceiling to the floor, with desk, task chair and computer hidden from general view. Creating a sacred space for reading, writing or painting is a good idea as it psychologically divides the activity from the rest of your life.

Houses in close proximity to parks tend to have a better yin–yang balance. If you live in the heart of the city, make the effort to visit the park to retrieve some balance for yourself.

Roads and railways

As conductors of Qi through an environment, roads can significantly transform where you live. Fast-moving Qi travels along straight urban roads; residents here often feel agitated and unable to relax. The same principle applies to houses at the end of long T-junctions or at busy intersections. Tall shrubs and plants on the boundary will slow down Qi, and can help restore some balance.

Always check the local transport patterns before purchasing or renting a home. Visit at different times of the day. Steady but not fast traffic on curving roads near your home can be beneficial. The best location is where Qi meanders – in the inner bend of a river or road.

The visual impact of an overpass can not only can change a home, it can conduct Qi away from the area, greatly affecting the fortunes of those living at eye level or underneath the overpass. Those living under an overpass should place lights on the corners of the house to symbolically lift the overpass. A home here may feel oppressive and depleted of energy. Similarly, trains carry Qi away, while subway trains are destabilizing, particularly if they are below the home. Residents of apartments overlooking a busy road should place a mirror outside their home to deflect the problem. Alternatively, colored glass in the windows facing the road will help block the unattractive view while allowing light in.

Above: Many warehouses that have been converted to contemporary living spaces still have their trademark high ceilings, vast windows and not a dividing wall in sight, making it difficult to "ground" the energy. Use screens, curtains, cushions or color to create boundaries between spaces; the result is cozier, and more intimate.

Above: This inner-city warehouse has ample cozy, comfortable yin areas. Colorful curtains have been used to separate the living and dining area from the kitchen and bathroom areas. Soft furnishings, plants and appropriate lighting have also been used to enhance, divide, and balance the space.

Country and Coastal Living

These days the pursuit of lifestyle has become an art. Combine this with a change in work structure, increased reliance on technology and a willingness to sacrifice accessible urban commodities for time commuting. People move to country or coastal locations because they're desirous of a peaceful, leisurely paced, relaxed life – there are walks, better air quality and outdoor space. The downside may include isolation and traveling distances, as well as natural disasters such as flooding or fires.

Evidently, energies in the countryside or by the sea are different from those in urban environments, but they are equally powerful. When we carefully position or choose a home within the natural features of the landscape, we can draw on the protection of those features to nourish us.

According to the traditional principles of Feng Shui, a sheltered position contained by trees, a hill or a mountain is ideal, particularly in remote areas, where protection from the elements is important. The perfect site is the classic Feng Shui arrangement of the four animals (see pages 12 and 27), but if it's flat where you live, large trees or buildings can serve as protectors.

Road access is important in rural areas, but as with urban living, it is considered inauspicious to live close to a major road. Beware of narrow country lanes, which funnel Qi swiftly and afford no relief for the driver. A property at the end of a narrow road is best remedied by tall overhanging trees, which assist with protection from the elements. Avoid planting high banks of hedges along a narrow road which leads to your home, as Qi will be fast-flowing. In the country, Qi is usually well balanced, but try to select a property that is not near areas where intensive farming methods are used (or planned).

Energy is good near water, particularly near slow-flowing rivers which meander through the countryside. Streams or ponds attract wildlife and accumulate good Qi. Living by the sea gives us a sense of well-being. But many peninsulas are difficult, because Qi dissipates in the winter when the environment is hammered by the elements.

Above: Creating a private outdoor area where you can take "time out" – to relax, read or drink tea – is an important element of modern living. You don't necessarily have to reside in the country or by the coast to achieve this. This private retreat, for example, was created on the rear veranda of an urban home.

Above: The perfect arrangement for a site or a home is one where the four mythical animals are present. These animals are represented by a sheltered position contained by trees, a hill, or a mountain or a body of water across the front of the home. If none of these elements are present and the area surrounding the home is flat, a Feng Shui trick is to apply substitute "protectors" such as large trees, hedges, plants, pots, buildings or stonewalls covered in creepers or fences.

Left: Good gardening, like conscious, sensitive living, is auspicious Feng Shui. The general rule of thumb for gardening auspiciously is to ensure there's a gentle flow of energy, balance and healthy plants (which have broad, not spiky, leaves). Keep weeds at bay and remove any dead or diseased plants. Remember, by carefully positioning or choosing a home that is set within the natural features of the landscape, we can draw on its protection to nourish us. But if you live in an apartment or the heart of the city, it's up to you to create your own life-giving garden. Whether you live in the country or the city, there's no excuse not to have plants!

Entrances

The last thing any of us want, after a hard day working or traveling, is to return home to a dark, unwelcoming environment. Returning to a nurturing sanctuary, approached through a pleasant, meandering and well-lit environment, is ideal. And of all the Feng Shui considerations, the entrance approach to and direction of the front door are the most important. The approach to the home is representative of the image we present to the world, and can be indicative of the view we have of ourselves. Living in an apartment may limit what you can do, but the same principles apply. It's necessary to distinguish your own special part of the block. Make it unique, and be creative – use a colorful doormat, introduce plants, lights, mirrors. And inside, your home should be as welcoming as the approach.

Having a place of transition between the outside world and your personal space is a tradition followed in China and Japan. This place of transition is located at the main entrance of your home. It's a place to stop, rest, take a deep breath and remove your shoes. Try to create such a space, perhaps through the use of screens or curtains. This will allow you to leave the pressures of the day behind and unwind. Also, walls opposite an entrance will obstruct it, doing little to create positive Qi.

Front gardens quickly fill up with stagnant energy unless we're careful. We need to avoid placing garbage cans in the front garden, as they can seriously affect how we feel when we return home. Place them instead behind a hedge or fencing, toward the back or side of the house. If there is no alternative to locating the garbage can in the front garden, try concealing it with an attractive pot plant, interesting garden sculpture or tall terracotta pot filled with river pebbles or shells.

The location and direction of entrances and doorways are believed to strongly influence individual fortunes, and fortunes of your household and/or workplace. Feng Shui practitioners believe enhancing your personal wealth can be facilitated by checking whether an entrance is auspicious for you. If the main entrance is not located in your best direction, check for another entrance you can use. If this is not an option, you can still increase the positive energy flowing into your home – keeping the entrance to your home well lit will clarify your future, and fixing a broken doorbell may prompt job offers and enhance your social life.

Above: In Feng Shui, the grander the main door, the more auspicious the home. However, beware of doors that are out of proportion with the home. Solid doors are preferable to transparent or see-through doors, and wood is better than glass or steel.

Below: Wind chimes or crystals hanging inside the front door help remedy the taboo of visitors seeing the back door from the entrance. It is considered impolite (and bad Feng Shui) to show your guests the back door as soon as they arrive. If wind chimes or crystals don't appeal to you, a folding screen, small wall or plant will also do.

Paths

Straight paths from the street to the front door conduct too much Qi, leaving us with little time to unwind. Ideally, paths should meander gently through a leafy, well-lit garden. This serves as a clear distinction between work and home, allowing us time to relax. Paths and entrances in urban environments are often cluttered with cars. Walkways and lanes are often narrow, dark and constrained – they may mirror our approach to life.

Front doors

The front door is regarded as the "mouth" of the home, because it is where energy comes into your home. In Feng Shui, the direction of the front door is important; ideally, the door should also be unpretentious, practical, and in proportion. A front door which captures the sun will help you capture fame, fortune, and longevity. A view from your front door through to your back door is bad Feng Shui, as showing your guests the back door as soon as they arrive is considered impolite. It also means that Qi will run straight through, without having the chance to move around your home. A crystal or wind chimes hanging inside the front door will help remedy this situation; a folding screen, small wall or plant would also do. The front door shouldn't line up with or face a bathroom door or a mirror – a mirror will deflect good Qi entering the house, sending it directly out again. Make sure the front door isn't rusty or squeaky, and that it is painted. Keep a porch light on at night even when you're away.

Far Left: A front door which captures the sun is thought to help you capture fame, fortune, and longevity. Also, as with this home, it is important to keep the entrance clutter free and to keep fresh flowers there. Be scrupulous with the repair of doors throughout your home, especially the front door, as it's an indicator of energy flowing throughout the house. Keep doors freshly painted in bright, vivid colors.

Left: Placing a potted plant or a container of flowers on either side of the front door is good Feng Shui. It's even better if they're jade "money" plants – these are thought to bring wealth and long life. Plants are great poison arrow diffusers and can deflect negative Qi at the front of your home.

Clearing Your Space

Removing Clutter

The art of space clearing is derived from tribal customs and Feng Shui techniques, including those from Tibet, India and Native American tribes.

Over the centuries, various elements have been applied to clear energy from a room, including melodious sounds such as crystal singing bowls, Tibetan cymbals or metal chimes. Drumming, clapping, purification with salt water and the application of incense are just a sample of other methods. While each of these various methods differ in some respects, the essential elements remain. Space clearing involves removing negative energy and increasing beneficial energy, while artfully and sensitively placing objects so as to increase the flow of Qi.

Spring is one of the traditional times for renewing your energies and those of your home – hence the term "spring-cleaning." The increase in the sun's energy at this time of year is reflected in increased creativity and activity. By removing clutter and the stale energy of winter from your home, you are creating space for new, revitalizing energy.

Feng Shui is not only concerned with obvious clutter; it also focuses on hidden untidiness in cupboards, on shelves, in drawers, under beds. Left cluttered, these spaces can cause stagnation and blocked Qi, resulting in an uncomfortable, rarely used room.

Clutter is a state of mind – when you clear out the clutter in your home, you clear out the clutter in your life. A messy home or work environment can indicate attachment to the past or fear of the future. Clutter encourages stagnant Qi and can make the occupants of the house depressed. The more space you have within your environment, the more space you will have in your life for new beginnings.

The hallway

The hallway sets the tone for the rest of the house, so look at it as a guest would. Is there somewhere to hang your coat, place your hat, put your shoes? What about umbrellas? Putting a hat stand in the entrance area, or hooks along the wall, will make your homecoming easier. Consider a wooden or woven sea grass box – perfect for shoes or gardening gloves.

Opposite: Disorganization and a lack of focus in personal relationships are thought to be the underlying reasons for clutter in the bedroom. But remember, Feng Shui is concerned not only with obvious clutter, it also focuses on hidden untidiness in cupboards, on shelves, in drawers and under beds. It's also good Feng Shui practice to ensure furnishings and lights on either side of the bed are balanced in size, proportion and color.

Below: Because the entrance and hallway set the tone for the rest of the house, make sure there is somewhere to hang coats, place umbrellas, put your shoes. Is there somewhere to put newspapers, bills, junk mail? Clutter is a state of mind – when you clear out the clutter in your home, you clean out the clutter in your life.

Above: Pictures, objects and ornaments in the living room are symbolic of the feelings of the family. To remove negative energy, clear some space. Don't allow clutter to build up on coffee tables, bookshelves, or magazine racks.

Above: The same living room is now much more conducive to conversing, relaxing with loved ones, and welcoming guests and friends. Space clearing has increased beneficial energy, and artfully and sensitively placing objects has increased the beneficial flow of Qi.

But if you're renovating or starting from scratch, try designing an inbuilt storage area in the entrance (make sure that the shelving is concealed). Hang a mirror on it to bring in the light or reflect outdoor views, but make sure it is to the side and not facing the door. Alternatively, consider a multipurpose modular piece of furniture with drawers, hooks, a mirror, a place to put the phone. But remember to keep it clutter free and tidy. The same rule applies with dying or dead plants – remove them and replace with fresh ones.

The bedroom

The bedroom is our personal sanctuary from the world, so it's important that we get it right. The placement of furniture, electrical devices and pictures in the bedroom can have a strong impact on our emotional life and health. So keep electrical appliances to a minimum, consider shifting them out altogether, or opt instead for battery-operated devices. If that's not possible, cover them with a yin-colored cloth.

Clutter in the bedroom is a no-no, as it's thought to reflect disorganization and a lack of focus in personal relationships. Remove all images of yourself on your own. Remove all pictures of, and objects given by, past partners you have been in unhappy relationships with. Give away or throw away clothes which no longer fit. Separate your current wardrobe into different seasons and store those which are not required at the moment. Make sure your dressing table is clear of empty or unused bottles and containers. It is believed that replenishing supplies in empty bottles or containers will dispel feelings of loneliness. Banish unread books, waste bins, notebooks and anything to do with work.

Avoid garish, wild prints and designs on fabric or walls. Storage in your bedroom, particularly above eye level, may result in a constricted feeling in your head and eyes.

For those in pursuit of a good night's sleep, keep the space under your bed clear. It is a Chinese belief that having clutter under your bed means you are sleeping on the issues you're not willing to face.

Lastly, cover all mirrors in your bedroom. In Feng Shui, it is believed that your spirit rises as you sleep, and it will be disturbed by seeing itself in a mirror. Having no mirrors present is also good for rectifying an unhappy relationship or marriage.

The living room

The living room is a place to live, converse, relax with loved ones and welcome friends. It's also a place where discussions can erupt into arguments. It's important we try to disperse this destructive energy as soon as possible. And because the pictures, objects and ornaments are symbolic of the feelings of the family, ask yourself some questions. Are the pictures which decorate the walls of your living area harmonious? What are their associations? What sort of objects fill the room?

If you have a fireplace, keep it clean at all times. Televisions, VCRs and stereos should be placed at some distance from seating, due to their potentially harmful electromagnetic radiation. Consider concealing them in a cupboard with doors, so they can be hidden away when not in use. Don't let clutter build up on coffee tables or in magazine racks, and change magazines regularly. Check that the living room is not being hit by poison arrows – these can be created by angular furniture, corridors, the corners of internal walls or a neighboring roof line. If poison arrows are a problem, establish where they are being generated in order to soften their effect in your home. Remedy a problematic neighboring building or structure with stained or frosted glass in windows. Small side tables, settees or narrow bookcases can be installed in corridors which funnel Qi too vigorously.

Above: Here, the symbol of a fish, representative of life and good fortune, has been placed in the fireplace to diffuse powerful Fire energy. Displaying the fish symbol as a vase, as a painting or on a screen would be equally effective. Keeping a clean, clutter-free fireplace is very auspicious Feng Shui.

Left: In Feng Shui, the nature of clutter is thought to symbolize what you are feeling about your life. For example, empty jars or bottles reflect feelings of loneliness or emptiness; items stored under your bed represent issues you're not willing to face. What kind of clutter do you have in your home? Dirty laundry, cheap cosmetics or junk in your relationships corner? To carry out a Feng Shui clearing room by room, you need a compass, a grid and a rough room plan. These items help you establish which sectors of your room correspond to the various life aspirations (see pages 28–31). Sketch out your room plan, complete with furniture placement, and see where clutter is congregating.

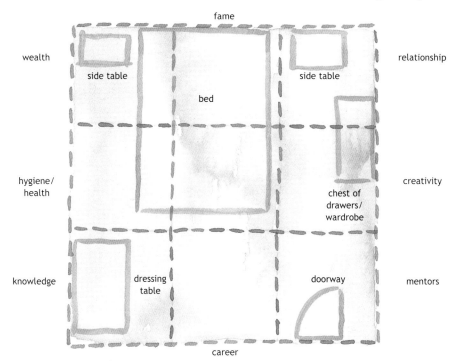

Above: Although there's a current fashion to hang pots, pans and kitchen utensils on beams or above kitchen work spaces, the Chinese consider this practice inauspicious Feng Shui, as it can create hard-hitting poison arrows.

Below: Here, overhead utensils have been removed and stored in appropriate storage drawers in the kitchen. In their absence, red Chinese lanterns have been added – red is a good color to stimulate the appetite and the lanterns create a barrier between the kitchen and the adjacent dining room.

The kitchen and dining space

Clearing clutter is also important in the kitchen and dining space. If you are planning a kitchen from scratch, or planning a renovation, make sure there's plenty of storage space – big pot drawers, pull-out corner cupboards, a walk-in pantry and cabinets for tucking away the microwave and the dishwasher. There's a current trend to display knives on walls – it's better Feng Shui to tuck them away safely or store them in a wooden block.

Hanging strips of garlic, onion or chili is not good, as dead plants create too much yin energy – store them in cupboards or vegetable racks. Hanging utensils from an overhead beam is also considered inauspicious, as it creates a lot of poison arrows. The kitchen operates best if it's kept clean and clutter free. It should be a yang area, so don't fill it with yin objects such as unpaid bills or old dried flowers.

In Feng Shui, the kitchen and dining rooms are symbols of your family's prosperity, abundance and wealth, so try to keep the Feng Shui flowing positively. Once you have eliminated the generation of negative energy, consider setting aside one full day for cleaning your kitchen from top to bottom and reorganizing it. Stock your pantry with your favorite ingredients. Chinese tradition says that the rice container should never be empty – always keep a well-stocked pantry and fridge.

The bathroom

The bathroom is for purification, so it should be clean, airy and simple. It should have good ventilation, effective lighting, privacy and little clutter. Remove anything which hampers these positive aspects. Set aside a day for reviving the energy of this room. Take out all clutter from drawers and cabinets. Determine what you do and don't need and consider how best to store the necessary items.

Make sure your storage area is concealed behind doors, a screen or curtains. Make sure the waste bin isn't overflowing. Remove silk, plastic or dried flowers. Don't allow damp to spread – hidden mold represents a hidden problem in your life. Remove sharp or angular furniture and replace it with soft, organic, round shapes. The bathroom is associated with a yin energy and because of its relationship to the element Water, the state of your bathroom is also symbolic of your wealth. Make sure the taps don't leak, as this symbolizes your wealth running away. Enliven the space with fresh smells, candles, plants and appropriately positioned mirrors.

The workspace

If you work from home, either occasionally or on a full-time basis, consider implementing a routine cleansing of your home office – it is a good idea to do this after a major project has ended, or before planning to attract new clients. Some freelance workers find they do this automatically, as they have an instinctive urge to "clear the decks" before new work comes in. In Feng Shui, it is believed that the act of clearing "old energy" encourages "new energy" to enter your life. Clearing your work space can be anything from tidying your files or tools to rearranging furniture. Make sure your office space is dust free – wipe down the tabletop. Tidy up books, files, tools and equipment and determine whether you need past files in the office or you can store them elsewhere. Overwhelming clutter in your work environment could lead to the inability to concentrate or work effectively. Try to avoid having your desk or office space in your bedroom – this will interfere with your sleep. If your work area cannot be situated outside the bedroom, ensure there's a barrier, such as a screen, to psychologically differentiate the opposing activities. Also, cover yang devices such as computers and printers with a cloth at night to create a restful, peaceful atmosphere.

Far Left: In Feng Shui, the kitchen and dining rooms are symbols of your family's prosperity, abundance and wealth, so keep Qi flowing positively in these areas. Stock your pantry with your favorite ingredients. In Chinese tradition, the rice container should never be empty, so always keep your kitchen well stocked. But equally important is having a neat pantry, not one which is crammed tight with old, unused containers and jars – ensure these are removed.

Left: Clearing clutter is important in the kitchen and dining areas. If you are planning a new kitchen or a renovation, make sure there's plenty of storage space – big pot drawers, pull-out corner cupboards, a walk-in pantry and integrated cabinets for tucking away the microwave, dishwasher and fridge.

Materials, Objects, and the Five Elements

Interpreting and balancing the elements plays a major role in the practice of Feng Shui and its application in home interiors. The elements also help identify the requirements of a Feng Shui makeover – we need to know where the most important associations are and how the five elements relate to the eight compass directions. Listed here are modern design equivalents and design suggestions in relation to each of the five elements.

Wood

The Wood element is associated with the southwest (wealth) and east (family) sectors of the home. It is also associated with the color green and tall, cylindrical shapes. To encourage financial luck or improve family relationships, place wooden furniture and decorative or other objects in the appropriate sector.

WOODEN FURNITURE: Footstools, dining chairs and tables, coffee tables, benches, bookcases, bedside tables, storage boxes, hat stands.

WOODEN FEATURES: Walnut screens, guitars, polished wooden floorboards, internal wall paneling.

BAMBOO, WICKER, RATTAN: In contrast to the Yang characteristics of highly polished wood, these materials tend to be yin and slow down Qi. Upholster furniture made from these materials in sumptuous fabrics – and add cushions – to create a striking balance.

SEA GRASS AND RUSH MATTING: Popular natural products, though difficult to clean. Good for coastal flooring, mats or furniture. Sea grass or woven hyacinth are available for almost all furniture pieces – lounges, beds, coffee tables, lamps, bedside tables, ottomans.

Above: Various types of the Wood element found in home interiors are shown in this image – the color green, a bamboo plant, a woven sea grass chair, wicker bowls, a hardwood floor. If the Wood element is placed in the appropriate sector of the home, it is thought to encourage healthy finances and improve family relationships.

Opposite: Interpreting and balancing the elements plays a major role in the practice of Feng Shui. It's undesirable to place the stove (Fire) next to the sink (Water), as these are opposing elements. Faced with no option in this kitchen, a wooden buffer was introduced between the two, to diffuse and ground the energies.

Above: Plants and flowers are in the Earth and Wood categories. Plants have potent Qi – they help harmonize energy in the home and circulate energy in disused corners, shelves, or on side tables.

Above: Not only is natural and artificial light – such as candles or lamps – associated with the Fire element, but also triangular, pyramid or pointed shapes. With the added benefit of this lamp's pointed shape, its Fire potency is increased. Added to the south sector of your room or home, a lamp, geometric shape or vibrant color will help you achieve greater public recognition, should you desire it.

PAPER PRODUCTS: Delicate paper screens, lampshades, pendant lights, floor lamps, transparent indoor and outdoor lanterns.

FLORAL PRINTS AND STRIPES: Wallpaper designs. Lampshades with floral motifs. Flowery or striped cushions, rugs, bedspreads. Curtains, upholstery, throws to enliven muted tones on armchairs. Cushions to soften armchairs, sofas or the floor.

RECTANGULAR SHAPES: Ottomans, freestanding rectangular lights, footstools, modular shelving or storage.

COLORS: Greens and blues.

ARTWORK: Containing plants, landscapes, gardens and flowers.

PLANTS AND FLOWERS: Both real and artificial – all plants are representative of the Wood element. Try using plants which clean the air and enjoy being indoors, such as peace lilies, Boston ferns or lady palms. Flowers enliven the senses as well as drawing energy to or lighting up a corner of a room.

Fire

The Fire element, which is associated with a south direction (fame and recognition), exudes a powerful and energizing yang energy. In the home, Fire is potently symbolized by the application of red, purple or bright pinks. All natural and artificial lights – candles, skylights, lamps, fireplaces, sunlight – fall into the Fire category. Triangular, pyramid, pointed and star shapes are associated with this element, as are geometric patterns or plants with pointed leaves. If you seek greater public recognition, add Fire energy to the south sector of your room or home.

PLASTICS, VINYL AND OTHER MANUFACTURED MATERIALS: Plastics and other manufactured materials fall into this category, as they have usually been produced using heat processes. The category includes vinyl tiles, plastic bowls and containers, synthetic cushions, rugs or fibers and plastic or synthetic bathroom curtains.

NATURAL AND ARTIFICIAL LIGHTING: This category includes all kinds of lighting. Try applying tall floor lamps in warm red tones – these can be further enhanced by using a red or purple globe. Chandeliers are particularly good Feng Shui. Use pendant lights and bedside and floor lamps. Also apply natural light from windows, skylights, fireplaces and burning candles.

ANIMAL PRODUCTS: This includes leather and wool. Leather lounges, cowhide rugs or wall hangings, wool and mohair rugs and throws, plus woven cushion covers, upholstery.

OBJECTS: A red or pink vase. Red scatter cushions for the floor or couch.

ARTWORK: Depicting sunshine, light, people or animals.

TRIANGULAR SHAPES: A triangular sculpture. Pyramids, geometric forms, zigzag patterns on fabrics, tablecloths, napkins, bedspreads or curtains.

COLORS: Warm red tones, vibrant oranges, purples, pinks.

PLANTS AND FLOWERS: Red roses, geraniums, begonias, bromeliads, poinsettias, plants with red berries, aspidistras.

Earth

Connected to both the southwest (relationships) and northwest (knowledge) sectors, this element is symbolized by earthenware objects. It brings harmony to a space. The nature of the element Earth is openness, closeness, and togetherness. It is strengthened by flowing lines, soft furnishings and objects. Try bringing nature into your environment (plants, flowers, water) to enhance the gentle aspects of this element. Earth colors are easy to pick – yellow tones, ocher, beige and terracotta. If you're keen to boost a relationship or your ability to absorb information or concentrate, place any of the objects or finishes listed below in the relevant sector in your room or house. Low, spreading plants or cube-shaped objects also do the trick.

BRICKS AND TILES: Brick paving in outdoor areas or internal feature walls is representative of earth. Try terracotta flooring, wall tiles or antique plaques throughout open-plan spaces. Tiles in bathrooms or kitchens. Splash backs.

CLAY, CERAMICS, PORCELAIN: Ceramic bowls or sinks, porcelain jars, clay pots. Ceramic figurines and sculptures.

STONE AND MARBLE: Marble flooring and finishes on features such as island benches in kitchens or vanities in the bathroom. Polished concrete floors. Stone bowls, plinths, plaques, fireplaces, feature walls and floors. Sculptures and statues. River pebbles.

FURNISHINGS: All furnishings or insertions in earthy tones.

SQUARES AND RECTANGLES: Low, wide, cube-shaped objects such as coffee tables or ottomans. Square or rectangular-shaped rooms.

ARTWORK: Containing landscapes.

COLORS: Yellow tones, ocher, terracotta, browns, beiges.

PLANTS: Sunflowers, slipper flowers, marigolds, daisies and other plants with yellow tones. Low, spreading plants.

Above: The Earth element is symbolized here by earthenware objects, which bring harmony into the home. Earth colors are yellow tones, ocher, beige and terracotta. If you want to boost a relationship, or increase your ability to absorb information and concentrate, place Earth elements, objects or tones in the relevant sector of your room or house. Earth elements are particularly good when applied to a home office or study.

Above: Metal is considered very yang, as hard, reflective surfaces make Qi flow faster. Reflective surfaces also suggest efficiency and action, making metal useful in the kitchen and in stagnant areas (such as the bathroom). When applied well, Metal can be a very effective Feng Shui tool – clocks, for instance, are considered very auspicious. Metal can be found everywhere around the home, from garden taps to lights in the driveway. Because it's a potent Feng Shui tool, take note of where metal is positioned in and around your home. Poor positioning could have adverse effects.

Metal

Hard, reflective surfaces make Qi flow faster; this makes metal very yang. The Metal element is associated with the west (children) and northwest (mentors). It is believed that placing metal objects in the west enhances the well-being or luck of your children. When metal is placed in the northwest, your ability to network will be enhanced. Apply crystals, white, gray, gold or silver-colored objects and spherical, round or dome shapes.

STAINLESS STEEL: Use as a surface in kitchens or bathrooms, or as kitchenware, including knives, colanders, saucepans, stove tops.

MATERIALS: Polished, hard, stone surfaces – including marble or granite – have the capacity to add Metal energy to a room.

Copper, brass, iron, and other metals: Metal tiles, pots, urns.

CRYSTALS AND GEMSTONES: Hang these in windows or apply in sacred spaces.

OBJECTS: Metal or silver sculpture. All metal objects. Coins, clocks, candlesticks, plates, photo frames.

SHAPES: Circles, ovals, arches, round shapes, domes.

COLORS: White, gray, silver, gold and pastels, applied to walls and soft furnishings, and as insertions such as cushions, rugs or other objects.

METAL: Money plants, oleander, jasmine, baby's breath.

Water

Water is usually associated with soothing qualities, but it can also be used to energize a space – or a specific area of your life. Water is associated with the north (career), but be sparing, as moving water can overstimulate Qi, which is exactly why fountains, aquariums and images of water are no good in the bedroom. Water stimulates Wood in the productive cycle, so a water feature, finish or object placed in the southeast sector can activate money luck.

REFLECTIVE SURFACES SUCH AS GLASS AND MIRRORS: Be careful where you apply mirrors or reflective surfaces, as too many mirrors in the home can create a sharp, bustling environment. Correctly applied, they are extremely beneficial. Also consider glass-front cabinets, stained glass, frosted glass and glass tiles.

OBJECTS: Glass vases, pots, sculptures, figurines.

WATER FEATURES: These include fountains, fish tanks, aquariums (with goldfish).

ARTWORK: Containing images of the sea, streams, ponds or fish.

SHAPES: Wavy, organic shapes.

COLORS: Black, gray and dark blue.

PLANTS AND FLOWERS: The Water element can be introduced by standing plant pots on blue or clear glass or in a glass vase.

Above: Water represents important aspects of life – wisdom, contemplation and healing; it stimulates and refreshes Qi energy. Introducing a water feature, a regularly watered plant or an aquarium in the home will enhance your career sector. Water is also strongly associated with money, so if you place it in your wealth area it will boost your finances and luck. Glass has depth and light, which is why its true home is Water. Here, an attractive water feature in a back garden combines two Water elements – glass and free-flowing water.

Element	Direction	Season	Condition	Emotion	Body	Color	Shape	Number
Fire	South	Summer	Heat	Joy	Heart Small intestines	Red Purple Pink	Triangular Pointy	9
Earth	Northeast Southwest Center	Late summer	Wet	Concentration	Spleen Stomach	Brown Yellow	Flat Low	2, 5
Metal	West Northwest	Autumn	Dry	Grief	Lungs Large intestines	White Silver Gold	Round	6, 7
Water	North	North	Cold	Fear	Kidney Bladder	Black Blue	Irregular Wavy	1
Wood	East Southeast	Spring	Wind	Anger	Liver Gallbladder	Green	Tall Column	3, 4

Color in the Home

Applying Color

More than just evoking feelings and affecting thoughts or behavior, color has the capacity to transform our lives. Individual colors can affect how comfortable we are in various environments, our moods, how we interact with others, even how others perceive us. If we examine our own personal use of color – what we wear – we can begin to see how this process works. Wearing hot pink will make us feel confident or emboldened; yellow, more cheerful or talkative; while black has the capacity to make us feel withdrawn or "shut off" from the world. Consider the emotional properties of color – are we green with envy, red with rage, sad or just feeling blue?

The same principles apply to manipulating and applying colors in the home. Color determines the ambience of a room and therefore our experience in it. Does the room make you feel energized or depressed? Can you relax there, concentrate or study there, have discussions there? The more we understand and explore how this process works, the more we can create spaces which work to our advantage.

Color and light

Light contains all colors, each with its own frequency. So when applying color, we're also working with light. Every space – each home, room, windowsill, courtyard – is different, and every space's light quality depends on many things. These include aspect, size, sources of natural and artificial light, decorative elements, materials and finishes. Light is reflected or absorbed, creating illusions of depth, movement, energy and size; dark colors absorb more light than lighter colors. Insertions of color in a room will create movement and energy in that area. And that's where Feng Shui steps in – apply a particular color to focus on a particular sector in your life and you will draw energy to that area.

It is worth noting that black is symbolic of the clean slate upon which you can apply the full color spectrum; white is a fresh canvas, evoking the symbolism of innocence. And from white and black, many hues and shades evolve. Yin is the blackness which absorbs all colors; yang is the whiteness which reflects them.

Above: Feng Shui tradition claims that people respond positively to defined spaces for life's defined activities – eating, cooking, sleeping, socializing, playing, working. Create barriers between spaces using colorful, bright screens – between bedroom/study, kitchen/dining room, hallway/bathroom, living room/children's play area. Why not design or paint your own?

Opposite: Apply color to focus on a particular sector in your life and you will draw energy to that area. Red, hot pink, and bright oranges are associated with warmth, passion, prosperity and the element Fire. These colors are excellent when used as accents, to enliven a room with energy, movement and spark. Red is perfect for activating the romance sector, but avoid using it in the kitchen or dining room.

Above: Using orange tones or objects in the kitchen or dining room is considered auspicious, as this color stimulates the appetite, and encourages sharing, nourishing and communication. If the dining room is located in the center of the house (an area associated with the element Earth), these positive characteristics will be even more pronounced.

Above: A decorative chair has been added to this home office — it adds a splash of color for mental stimulation and enhances the fame sector of the office. Because of their contact with the outside world and various electrical devices (computers, printers), home offices tend to be yang, so use bright colors sparingly and thoughtfully. A backdrop of earthy tones in the home office will create an atmosphere of stability and elegance.

The color spectrum

WHITE: White is the yang which reflects all colors. It's symbolic of new beginnings and purity of thought. It's clean, pared-back and vibrant when applied correctly; if not, it can be stark and cold. Apply white freely in bathrooms and kitchens, but avoid using it in children's bedrooms and dining rooms, where its negative associations become evident.

BLACK: Black is the yin which absorbs all colors. If applied excessively, it can be overbearing, depressing, dark. Surprisingly, it is not bad Feng Shui when applied in teenagers' bedrooms or in master bedrooms, but use black as an accent, not as a feature. Avoid using it in young children's rooms, studies or living rooms.

RED: Dominant, stimulating red can reduce the size of a room or increase the size of objects. It is excellent as an accent color to enliven a room with energy and movement, but don't apply it with abandon. It's bad Feng Shui if applied in the kitchen or dining room, but it's perfect for activating the romance sector of your house or room. Red is associated with warmth, passion and prosperity.

ORANGE: A powerful color, orange encourages communication. Think of the sun. Think of fire. Use orange in living rooms, dining rooms and hallways, but not in constrained rooms or in the bedroom. Orange is associated with concentration and intellect. Its negative force is rebellion, so use it sparingly. Use it as an accent color against monochromatic backgrounds.

YELLOW: Associated with intellect and enlightenment, yellow stimulates the brain and aids digestion (one reason it's so good in the kitchen). Positive qualities include optimism and decisiveness; negative qualities are rigidity and exaggeration. Try applying a feature wall in yellow in the kitchen, or simply using a sunny yellow tablecloth or napkins.

GREEN: A symbol of growth and harmony, green is restful, refreshing and balanced. Green is excellent in bathrooms, therapy rooms or in areas for growing plants. Avoid applying it in living spaces, as it may encourage negative qualities such as deceit and envy.

BLUE: Peaceful and soothing, blue is linked to spirituality, mystery and patience. Negatives include suspicion and melancholia. Apply blue in meditation rooms, bedrooms and therapy rooms, and as means of enlarging spaces, but not in family rooms, dining rooms or studies.

PURPLE: Purple encourages vitality. It is dignified and regal. Positive associations are passion and motivation; negatives are mournfulness and force. It is excellent for bedrooms and meditation rooms, but not for bathrooms or kitchens.

PINK: Pink is linked to purity of thought – it has the positive association of happiness and romance, and no negatives. It is suitable for bedrooms, and for activating the romance sector of your room or home, but not for kitchens or bathrooms.

BROWN: Brown suggests stability and weight. Its positives are elegance and safety; its negatives are dinginess, depression and aging. It is excellent for studies, but not bedrooms. Apply it sparingly and thoughtfully. Some of its more earthy tones and hues are great for the living room. Apply with accents of more dominating colors, such as red.

Above: These Vietnamese lanterns are a colorful, stimulating addition to the hallway of an inner-city home. Hallways and entrances often set the tone for the rest of the house, so they should be brightly lit and colored.

Hallways/entrances

Hallways and entrances play a pivotal role within the home, often setting the tone for an entire house. Striding into a light, brightly colored hallway can be inviting and seducing, while a dark, dingy, cluttered hallway can be depressing. The hallway imprints our homecoming. Yellow is a perfect color here, as it is optimistic and decisive. Try a bright yellow paint, or mix it with white for a softer lemon – also, combine the paint with mirrors, to increase light. Place daffodils or lilies on a side table. Try a yellow ottoman which doubles as storage. What about a yellow umbrella stand? Orange is also good, as it's powerful and cheerful. If an entire orange wall is not your cup of tea, try combining it as a feature against a pale gray background. Paint the skirting boards, or the handrails on the stairwell, orange. Paint your own canvas – a sunset or field of flowers. But don't do all these things at once!

The bedroom

As the bedroom is predominantly a place of rest, romance and rejuvenation, it should be predominantly yin. Purple, pink, blue and green are excellent bedroom colors, each with its own impact and mood-enhancing qualities. Try a sumptuous silk bedspread in plum or deep purple – not only will it incite passion, but it is also dignified, regal and good Feng Shui. Scatter the bed with plump pink, lilac or white cushions. For a softer look, consider a pink mohair rug over a cappuccino-colored bedspread and crisp white sheets. For a dramatic look, use black, but be light-handed, as black can be oppressive. Use it as an accent or highlight in prints, lampshades, sleek bedside tables or cabinets. The color orange is not conducive to the intimacy of the bedroom, as it's too mentally stimulating and powerful. And a word of warning: avoid peach. "Peach-Blossom Luck" is a famous concept in China, pertaining to a husband or wife with a roving eye. Apply peach in your bedroom and you're asking for trouble if you're married! Lastly, don't forget the romance sector in the bedroom – activate it with two red candles, poetry and images of you with your loved one.

Children's bedrooms

White, despite its innocent associations, is bad news in children's bedrooms, where its stark and cold connotations blossom. Children love to be in a warm, secure environment – so opt for warm blues, pink, purple or pastels instead. Try wallpaper with fun motifs (select them with your child), hang mobiles, add bright screens to create a barrier which divides

Above: Light contains all colors, each with its own frequency. So when we're applying color, we're also working with light. And every space's light quality will be particular to that space – it will depend on many things, including size, aspect, objects, materials, finishes and natural and artificial light sources. These bottles of vinegars and chilies enliven the energy in an otherwise stagnant, disused corner of a country kitchen.

Opposite: Ensure the bedroom remains a special place of escape, rejuvenation, rest, romance. Keep it clutter free. Create sacred spaces. Yin colors are the most effective; try purple, pink, blue or green – each is restful and conducive to the affairs of the bedroom. A chaise longue placed in the bedroom for relaxing on will assist in creating an atmosphere for retreat.

Above: Animals and their symbolism are deeply rooted within Chinese culture. Pets are considered Feng Shui luck symbols, but traditionalists still consider it necessary to make sure that the color and pattern of pets' bedding is in harmony with the elemental energy of their sleeping position.

Above: Color is especially useful in dark corners and plain undecorated areas. Here, worn-out decking is brought to life with vibrant cushions.

Opposite: Though dark furnishings, leathers and wood combined together are elegant, where there is no relief the result can be gloomy. To remedy bad Feng Shui, invigorate areas such as this with splashes of color. A cushion with a hot pink trim was all it took to add spark to this handsome leather couch.

the play area from the sleep area. If the child has not chosen the colors, select shades and hues to reflect the child's personality – cooler ones to balance an active child and brighter ones to stimulate an introverted character. Equally, red or orange is not suitable for children's bedrooms, as both colors are too mentally stimulating and may make it difficult for children to relax at night. If your child loves these colors, use them as accents; for example, in cushions and toy sets. Should these colors be unavoidable, cover the dominantly colored areas with a yin cloth – blue or purple – at night. Applying black in a teenager's bedroom is permissible, but only as an accent color. Avoid it in young children's rooms. Its associations could be too overbearing or oppressive.

The living room

As a conversation area, the living room needs to be more yang than yin. Orange and bright tones in the living room encourage lively communication and interaction with family, loved ones and guests. This space is best when it's welcoming and energized. If painted in a single color, small areas of stimulation – such as brightly colored sculptures, artwork, flowers or tapestries – are necessary to keep the energy moving. And in conjunction with color, allow as much natural light in as possible. Try soft tangerine or ocher armchairs, an ottoman upholstered in terracotta to either sit on or put your feet up on. For the brave, try a wild orange shag-pile rug or comfortable beanbag against a more tonal backdrop. Avoid using green in the family room, as it may encourage its negative qualities – envy and deceit. Equally, black is no good, and blue can drain the color and energy from a living space. Too much dark brown will feel sluggish and depressing. Try bright wall hangings, pictures, tapestries or rugs to compensate if there is a lot of dark furniture (yin).

The kitchen and dining area

Places for sharing and nourishing, the kitchen and dining areas in your home are great locations for yellow and orange walls, trims or insertions. Particularly if the dining room is located in the center of the house, an area associated with the element Earth. As a general rule, colors in these areas should be predominantly yang, positive colors – although red could be too domineering. Softer shades and hues of red or pink can be applied; a red and white checked tablecloth, a bowl of red apples, salmon-colored napkins, a red sculpture or vase on a sideboard. But use it sparingly.

Strictly speaking, a bold red is not the most suitable color for dining rooms or kitchens. Neither are blue, pink or purple, which are best kept for the bedroom. White can be applied in kitchens, but it is not suitable in dining rooms. The solution to all this? A clean, fresh, white kitchen with wooden countertops in a sumptuous hardwood, with terracotta walls and earthy furnishings. Fabrics could be in lemon check, with bold cushions in a persimmon. Use daffodils with abandon. Another good option for the kitchen is green, since the Wood element, represented by green, supports Fire and is supported by Water, both of which will inevitably be in use in the kitchen (Fire = oven; Water = sink and refrigerator).

The bathroom

In Feng Shui, an auspicious bathroom combination is white and green – white is pure and clean, and green is restful and refreshing. The use of green removes any possible negatives which may result from the application of white. A blue bathroom is also soothing and contemplative, a great place to unwind or take long baths or showers. If the toilet is in view (bad Feng Shui), try applying a modular glass screen, an alcove or shelving. Yellow, purple and pink are unsuitable colors in the bathroom. If these colors are present, try repainting in a more suitable color scheme. Go for a blue tiles, detailing, materials, finishes. Enhance with pale blue towels, wooden blinds and glass bottles along the windowsill; hang a crystal and make the space dance with light. Images of the sea, fish or mermaids are also good.

The home office or study

While brown has many negative associations in the home – including in the bedroom, where it can be stifling and oppressive – it is an excellent choice for the home office or study. Brown suede wallpaper can look great. An elegant antique desk in walnut will stabilize the space. Black is too oppressive and weighty in a study and can be psychologically depressing. If the study is a small room, stay away from orange. Equally, green is not ideal for a study environment – although the use of plants will bring balance, adding yin to the yang of electrical devices such as computers and printers. Blue in this environment is too contemplative and serene. The home office tends to be more yang than a study, as it has more contact with the outside world. Look at which areas you seek to improve and focus on these areas, adding a splash of color to brighten the space – a red lampshade, for example, might be just the mental stimulation you need.

Opposite, top left and top right: This plain, undecorated corner of a stainless steel kitchen countertop with an old wooden chopping board is brought to life with an orange glass bowl, a reflective tray and ceramic vases. The result creates much more impact and increases the positive Qi in that stagnant corner.

Bottom left and bottom right: As well as being inauspicious Feng Shui, this empty platter on an antique table in a country dining room looks dull and lifeless. The bowl of fruit not only adds a spark of color, it instantly diffuses negative Qi associated with "emptiness." The dining room represents a family's abundance, wealth and prosperity, so displaying food or images of food is very good Feng Shui. Filling empty bowls, bottles and platters with beautiful objects, fruit, pebbles, crystals, rocks or shells is also a good idea.

Above: When renovating or revamping a home, exposing beams in the ceiling is a common contemporary design technique. In some parts of the world, people go to great lengths (in planning and financial outlay), to create homes, restaurants or hotels with rustic, skeletal appeal. Unfortunately, according to Feng Shui principles, exposed or low beams are thought to be oppressive, posing an obstacle to business, wealth or growth. Beams are not conducive to free-flowing Qi.

Opposite: Angular or linear columns or pillars in the home have the potential to "cut" sharply into the energy of the home, creating poison arrows. Applying modern cures to soften their presence is suggested. First, make sure the space around the column or pillar is not cluttered. Place a plant at the base to soften their appearance, or try wrapping them in fabric or covering them with mirrors to make them "disappear."

Feng Shui Cures

Beams, Columns, and Pillars

Where major structural work has taken place, the contemporary home often has exposed supporting pillars, columns or beams. While exposing them is a common design practice, the bad news in Feng Shui is that they're not conducive to free-flowing Qi. Often angular, linear and "cutting," they are potential poison arrow enhancers, best neutralized through the use of Feng Shui cures.

The Chinese believe that exposed or low beams are oppressive, posing an obstacle to wealth, growth and business. The higher the beam, the better – but always ensure that their height is in proportion to the rest of the house. Equally, protruding corners and columns are structural taboos. Modern apartment spaces often contain these, particularly if the space has been created by converting or dividing a large, older-style home. If you know where the structural beams are in your apartment, it's best to move furniture away from under them. A beam across an opening between two rooms may block Qi, and a beam running down the center of a marital bed (veritably dividing it) may cause a rift and separate the couple. Over the stove or dining area, beams are thought to hamper the fortunes of the family. And a beam over a desk may hinder the creative flow.

Decorative plaster ceilings with recessed lighting also generate poison arrows. Ceilings should, ideally, be flat. Introduce roses or other organic patterns instead, but avoid sharp, geometric lines.

Angular columns or pillars in the home block the free flow of Qi, "cutting" into the energy of the home. If they can't be avoided, it's best to accommodate living space around them, applying modern cures to soften their presence.

Modern cures: beams, columns, and pillars

By simply shifting a bed, armchair or desk from under an overhead beam, its associated problem can be relieved. Alternatively, try applying uplighting underneath beams, to provide the illusion of lifting them. It's important to camouflage or soften the negative Feng Shui of protruding corners, sharp angles and columns in the home. To this end, plants are excellent, particularly creepers with broad, round leaves. Similarly, lighting dark corners or decorating them with plants encourages Qi to circulate.

Hanging a wind chime also blunts the cutting edge of a corner. But make sure that the chime has hollow rods – there's a Chinese principle which claims that Qi is forced through the rods, and the melodious sounds thus produced make for auspicious Qi.

For the domestically ambitious, wrap the column with floor-to-ceiling mirrors to help make the column "disappear." The traditional cure for a beam across an opening between two rooms is to hang a bamboo flute, but hanging crystals or bells may also be appropriate. Small, light-colored objects are best. And avoid large, dark, heavy objects.

If your bedroom has exposed beams, try a four-poster bed to match the ambience. The canopy may afford some protection, but be careful and avoid steel – use a "lighter" option, such as wood, bamboo or sea grass woven around a timber frame. Soft curtains, or a mosquito net, might also provide an answer.

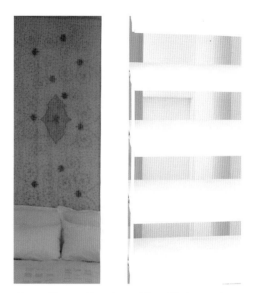

Above: It's considered good Feng Shui to make sure that rooms are well ventilated and filled with light. Be careful about how you dress your windows – blinds, such as those shown here, prevent access to views, and slatted blinds send cutting Qi into the room.

Below: Curtains, an alternative to slatted blinds, were added to this sun-filled bedroom. Make sure that curtains are kept open during the day, as keeping them closed can be associated with depression and vulnerability. Also, beware of windows which only open halfway – they restrict the amount of Qi entering a room.

Doors and Windows

Earlier we noted that front doors and entrances play a pivotal role in determining the quality of Feng Shui experienced in the household. The good news is, front doors and doors within the home are among the easiest things to adjust. The main elements to consider are their alignment and relationship to each other. It is considered inauspicious Feng Shui, for example, to place doors sequentially, particularly if one is the front door and one the back door. The Chinese claim it is bad manners to show guests the back door upon arrival. With doors positioned in this manner, negative Qi funnels too quickly through the home and positive Qi doesn't have a chance to circulate.

Doors are representative of our freedom, but they're also our barrier and protection from the world. The grander the main door, the more auspicious the home, it is believed. But beware of doors that are out of proportion to the home. Solid doors are preferable to transparent or see-through doors. And wood is better than glass or steel.

Too many windows in the dining room is inauspicious, since the aim is to gather Qi around a dining table and food prepared for loved ones.

Windows, which act as our eyes to the world, are important. But too many windows can create excessive yang, and too few can restrict the flow (excessive yin). Windows are best when they have a view of the outside world. Blinds, which prevent access to a view, are no good, while slatted blinds send cutting Qi into the room. Avoid closing curtains during the day, as they are associated with depression and vulnerability. Opt for sunlight instead – a much cheerier option. Beware of windows which only open halfway, as they restrict the amount of Qi entering a room. Ideally, windows should open fully and outward.

For those of us who don't have the luxury of manipulating the style of, or the view from, our windows, creating a window-box filled with herbs or plants could be the answer. By placing a window-box on the windowsill, we are filling our homes with the nurturing Wood energy of growing plants, while transforming a bleak outlook.

Modern cures: doors and windows

Instead of drawing curtains during the day, try experimenting with other solutions, such as large plants or colored or frosted glass. Whether in the bedroom or living areas of your home, these elements will enhance privacy and add energy to the space. While it is comforting to be reassured the world can't peer in, the aim should be to see out as much as possible.

As with light and privacy, airflow is another important Feng Shui consideration. If airflow is not an option in your bedroom, apply a small water feature containing oils. Hanging crystals from a beam or window is also a good idea.

Be scrupulous with the repair of doors throughout your home – especially the front door, as it's an indicator of energy flowing through the house. Make sure they don't squeak, creak or have broken latches. Keep a wedge or doorstop close by so they don't slam. Keep doors freshly painted in bright, vivid colors. A colorful doormat is also a good idea.

Where there are two or more doors facing each other in a row, break up the perspective by hanging low lights, positioning semi-circular tables, or placing broad-leafed plants between the doors to slow down Qi.

Chinese hand-painted furniture is another creative way to slow down Qi in problematic areas of the home. This furniture is not only elegant, the whimsical images are good Feng Shui. The hand-painted scenes usually depict cultural life in rural China, with figures at social gatherings, operatic events, in villages, and on horses. Try using lacquered armoirs, chests, screens or consoles.

Far Left: This old stable, which has been converted into a home, has ample natural light flooding in from overhead skylights, but keeping the door closed throughout the day means its residents miss out on pleasant views and a sunny aspect.

Left: Because the owner is keen to maintain privacy, but still have the luxury of good views, the door is kept ajar during the day (weather permitting) and fabric used as a fluid, transparent screen. The aim with Feng Shui in the home – while maintaining privacy, good ventilation and access to light – is to be able to see out as much as possible.

Edges, Corners, and Slanting Walls

Above: Families in constrained houses often convert attic spaces into rooms. The result can be slanting walls and sloping ceilings, as shown above. Both are problematic for Feng Shui. Sleeping or working under a slope depresses personal Qi – it reduces the regenerative power of sleep and inhibits creative working processes.

Below: Should a sloping ceiling be unavoidable in your home, apply mirrors, positive images, plants and rounded furniture and introduce light where possible. Using up-lights or lamps will create the illusion of lifting the slope.

While many contemporary designers and architects use sharp angles, jutting corners and slanting walls in their work, these are unfortunately problematic for Feng Shui. Conversions, similarly, can result in inauspicious structural details that cause discomfort or an inexplicable uneasiness for the occupants by affecting the free flow of Qi. The golden rule is: wherever Qi flow in a room is disrupted, difficulties may occur.

Edges of furniture pointing at us have the potential to make us feel uncomfortable, as can the edges of shelves, fireplaces and alcoves. Where there are sharp edges or angles in the home, we should always attempt to soften them, to diffuse the negative energy created by 'poison arrows.' Diffusing this negative energy is the cornerstone of living in a harmonious environment. And be aware of dark corners in a room: energy here will be stagnant, stale, lifeless – certainly not the sort of energy you want to encourage in your home! Plants, lights or colors are an excellent way to lift this negative energy. Alcoves with shelving or bookcases in close proximity to dark corners are also good Feng Shui, as they help prevent the areas becoming stagnant. Make sure, however, that the shelving or bookcases are not overflowing – leave some space. Keeping these areas clean and clutter free will result in good Qi flow.

Expanding families in constrained houses often convert attic spaces into rooms – children's bedrooms, home offices, sewing rooms, libraries or studies. The result can be slanting walls and sloping ceilings. Sloping ceilings can create a visual imbalance in the room and sleeping or working under a slope depresses personal Qi. These areas do little to assist the regenerative process of sleep or creative processes through the day – they are best used for play rooms or hobby rooms.

Modern cures: edges, corners, and slanting walls

The aim is to soften sharp or cutting edges in the home. Plants are one solution, fabric and mirrors another. Where possible, make edges or corners rounded, as this creates an entirely different, more organic feel. Keeping books in cupboards is a solution, but the pleasure of plucking a book from a shelf is then lost. Instead, use plants to soften shelf edges near where we sit and apply scatter cushions, soft rugs and ottomans.

The corners of these rooms are often dark, so it is a good idea to place something colorful there, such as a vase of silk flowers. Alternatively, use a water feature or floor lamp. Putting plants in dark corners will help move Qi around. Uplights and round tables with lamps or mirrors are other ways to expand dark corners.

Should a sloping ceiling be unavoidable, apply mirrors or lights, to help create the illusion of lifting the slope. Colorful, bright paint on the sloping walls can achieve the same effect. In which room does the problem exist? If it's the bathroom, try blue, green or white. For the study, a cheery lemon or a softly bright mustard brown can work wonders. Or if it's the hallway where the problem exists, try a splash of orange or a bold yellow. Another excellent solution is to fill in the sloping walls with built-in storage cupboards. And where skylights are installed to let light into attic conversions, make sure it is possible to see more than just sky. If the room is small, it is preferable that it be of conventional shape. Minimize the effect of slanting ceilings by painting them in light, neutral colors.

Far Left: Despite the elegance of this chair, this corner is rarely used by the residents of a modern inner-city apartment. Energy here has a feeling of neglect; it is stagnant and stale, with Qi unable to circulate freely.

Left: As an alternative, a much more comfortable yin option was created using a mirror, a lamp and a rug. These significantly expand this difficult corner noticeably. Always be careful with the size and position of mirrors – while they are powerful Feng Shui tools, if they are placed incorrectly they encourage negative Qi.

Natural and Artificial Lighting

The concept of light and dark is not foreign to any of us. In every culture and its mythology, white yang is representative of day, while dark yin is representative of night. Introducing light, whether natural or artificial, is one of the easiest ways to enhance and expand the energy experienced in your home. Symbolic of the Fire element, which produces Earth, enhances itself and causes Wood to blossom, light helps achieve balance and harmony in the home.

The application of bright lights in the entrance areas of the home is particularly important. Ideally, if your foyer is dark and cramped, these lights should be kept switched on. According to Chinese traditionalists, light is extremely useful for activating the southern, the southeastern, the eastern and the northeastern sectors. It can be applied in varying ways: floor lamps, candles, glass, crystals, windows, skylights, fireplaces. Remaining aware of how light comes into our homes enables us to arrange the interiors of our homes and the relevant activities, which change from room to room, appropriately. In an era where many of us live our lives out of synch with the natural rhythms of the sun, making sure we have the correct type and level of light in our homes is especially important for our health and well-being. The sun is representative of growth, renewal, and creativity. If you are currently lacking energy or inspiration in your life, perhaps you need to introduce more Fire energy in your home. But don't overdo it – Fire energy can be explosive and can provoke heated exchanges!

Below left: It's best to avoid high-tech or angular task lighting in rooms that are used for relaxing, such as the living room or the bedroom. They're best reserved for active (yang) spaces, such as the kitchen, home office or staircase. Where direct or task lighting is necessary, be selective – they are potential poison arrow creators.

Below right: Softer, moody lighting was selected for this living room. Other options include natural, neutral-colored or rounded lights, which bring an air of tranquillity and harmony to a room. To complement the relevant element of the corner that is being lit, make sure you give consideration to the general color and globe of the lamp.

Modern cures: lighting

Avoid high-tech lights and angular task lighting. Opt for natural, neutral-colored or rounded lights instead, as they lend an air of tranquillity and harmony to a room. In active spaces, such as the kitchen, home office or staircase, direct lighting may be necessary – just be selective. Uplights transform and illuminate dark areas, such as corners, alcoves or where there are beams, moderating their negative effect.

In rooms conducive to relaxing, such as living rooms or bedrooms, apply softer, moody lighting. Table lamps create soft pools of light. To complement the relevant element of the corner being lit, give equal consideration to the color of the lamp and the color of the light. For example, a dark blue lamp would be suitable for the northern sector, since blue equates with Water. Likewise, you could use a blue globe to activate this corner, which symbolizes career success.

Chandeliers are considered very auspicious – modest arrangements of cut glass are equally good. Try Venetian, antique, vintage, second-hand. When unlit, however, these lights have little Feng Shui value. Chandeliers are excellent when hung in the center of the home, which traditionally symbolizes the essence of the household. The center is symbolic of the Earth element, and Fire produces Earth. Colored and stained glass are effective and attractive ways to let in natural light. Crystals lift stuck and stagnant energy. Suspend any of these in a window and the light will shine through, creating rainbows on a wall or ceiling. A word of warning: crystals should be used with care. They have many facets, and these break light into tiny fragments – they can do the same to energies. A light hand here is best.

Candles, fireplaces and skylights add yang qualities to a yin area. Glare from the outside world should be softened by drapes, curtains and blinds.

Above: Chandeliers are considered very auspicious Feng Shui; modest arrangements of cut glass are equally good. This coolly elegant yet contemporary chandelier is based on a vintage style. When lit it significantly lifts stagnant energy in the home. Chandeliers are particularly effective when hung in the center of the home, which traditionally symbolizes the essence of the household. The center is symbolic of the Earth element, and Fire produces Earth.

Using Plants

With indoor plants or flowers, take heed of your own cultural traditions. What's considered lucky in one culture might be considered unlucky in another. What works in Tokyo may not work in New York or Morocco. While some cultures claim cacti or bonsai plants are bad luck, in others they're revered. Universally acknowledged, however, are the beauty, scent and potent Qi of plants, which restore positive equilibrium in the home.

Thriving, healthy plants, not sick ones, improve Feng Shui. When they are used in conjunction with the productive and destructive aspects of the five elements, plants can be even more effective. Depending on what life aspiration you wish to emphasize, they're powerful tools for activating the various corners of your home. For enhancing marriage or romance opportunities, the mou tan or peony is the traditional Chinese choice – activate the southwestern corner of any room by displaying a bunch.

The impala lily is thought to bring prosperity when placed in your living area, or near the front of a business. The jade "money" plant is thought to bring wealth and long life. Spider plants and poinsettias have been found to absorb electromagnetic radiation, making them ideal for the office.

Where there are sharp corners or angles in the home, plants are great poison arrow diffusers. Plants deflect the negative Qi of beams and columns; large plants slow Qi down in a corridor, hallway or at the front of the home. Filling the house with cut flowers creates welcoming Feng Shui. Artificial or silk flowers can be used, but it's not advisable to display dried flowers, as they signify death.

Modern cures: plants and flowers

Plants harmonize energy. For example, Fire and Water energy in kitchens is harmonized by placing plants between the sink and the stove. Plants drain excess water and yin energy in the bathroom. If your entrance is dull, red, yellow, or orange flowers will add vibrant yang colors. A painting or image of flowers is equally effective.

Arrange plants with broad, rounded leaves to conceal the angles and corners of bookcases, stairwells, or storage units. Avoid sharp, pointed leaves, especially in small environments. Buy a vibrant bunch of flowers to move energy in a dark corner.

Above: Filling the house with artificial, silk or cut flowers is welcome Feng Shui – just make sure that they have a healthy, abundant appearance. This artificial emerald bonsai is believed to be auspicious. Position indoor plants or flowers where there are sharp corners, angles, pillars or columns, as they will act as poison arrow diffusers.

Above: If you're not the world's best gardener, go for low-maintenance plants such as bamboo. Position bamboo where you want to introduce tree energy as an adjustment in your life. Consult your Bagua and consider which area you wish to invigorate. Bamboo's towering height and green color both embody energy moving upwards strongly and can provide effective results.

Mirrors and Reflective Surfaces

Above: When the chef in this kitchen cooks, his back is to the door. In order to be able to see anyone entering or leaving the kitchen, he has installed a mirror above the burners – this helps the flow of Qi and brings good fortune in business. However, much Feng Shui value has been lost here because of the poison arrows generated by knives and general clutter.

Above: Visible knives, open shelves, clutter, jutting corner cupboards and utensils hanging overhead should all be removed – they create poison arrows. The stove should not be placed under a window or skylight, because the beneficial energy from the stove will leave the house. Use all the burners on the stove regularly – this will keep the stove's energy flowing evenly, which will maximize your potential income.

Depending on where you place mirrors in your home, they can either deflect negative Qi or encourage positive Qi. There are three different kinds of mirrors – flat, concave and convex – each has its own qualities.

A convex mirror will diffuse negative Qi – this is good if you have an obstruction such as a building, telephone pole or wall outside your door. Though they are infrequently used, concave mirrors will help attract beneficial Qi into your home. A flat mirror has the benefit of providing a perfect mirror image – yin becomes yang, and bad Qi becomes good.

Beware of bad Feng Shui if mirrors are positioned incorrectly. Avoid placing them too low; for example, your face, rather than your chest, should be reflected. Beware of what mirrors reflect. Reflecting the main door, or any other door which opens to the outside, should be avoided. Avoid reflecting staircases, stoves or toilets. Don't hang mirrors opposite a door, window or brick wall, since they merely reflect the negative Qi. They are best when reflecting something pleasant, such as a view or garden – they then bring vibrant energy indoors to circulate through the home. The Chinese claim that mirrors opposite each other indicate restlessness – they are not recommended. Round or oval mirrors are preferable for bedrooms and bathrooms. Always have frames around mirrors, and try to have mirrors that can reflect your whole image. Don't hang mirrors directly opposite beds, windows or each other. Avoid hanging Bagua mirrors indoors – they create negative energy in the home. Keep your mirrors clean, unbroken and untarnished and be wary of antique mirrors in which the image is warped.

Mirrored tiles applied to walls can split or distort the Qi of the room or the energy of the person looking into them. On a larger scale, mirrored wardrobes with multiple doors also have this effect. Also, mirrors are best when framed, as they then contain the Qi of the image.

Modern cures: mirrors and reflective surfaces

Mirrors and reflective surfaces are extremely useful in constrained spaces, where they can double the size of the area. Where a house is irregularly shaped, mirrors can also be effective in recreating the missing space or "filling in" the corner. In awkward places, such as dark corners and at bends in passages, use mirrors to help Qi circulate and flow freely through the home. In long corridors, mirrors offer one method – plants and furniture are others – of slowing Qi down. Try positioning several mirrors in a staggered manner to reflect pleasant images.

Bagua mirrors are used to protect and deflect negative energies from the home. They are best used on front doors, or near the main entrance. Bagua mirrors represent yin energy – they should never be hung on the inside of the home, because they will negatively affect the energies of the occupants.

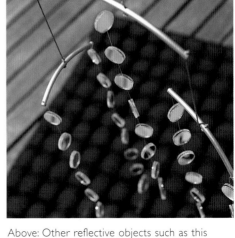

Above: Other reflective objects such as this mobile can be used in the same way as mirrors; reflective mobiles, metal pots, glass bowls, stainless steel objects or crystals are all beneficial.

Above: Where a home or room has a sector "missing," apply mirrors to cure the shape and energize the missing space.

Above: For this problematic L-shaped bedroom, a mirror has been used to symbolically "fill in" the missing area.

Above: Where a house or room is irregularly shaped, mirrors can "fill in" or expand the corner.

Above: In awkward places, apply mirrors to help Qi circulate and flow freely. Also try reflecting a bright painting or plant on the opposite wall.

Above: The position for this mirror is bad Feng Shui – it acts as a barrier, reflecting any positive Qi straight back out the door.

Above: The position for this mirror is good Feng Shui – it draws the positive Qi into and through the home, allowing it to circulate freely.

Traditional Feng Shui Remedies

Below: There are two reasons a fishtank is so powerful in the wealth corner of your room or home: not only does it have the element of water, but also the movement of fish. As the fish swim in the tank, they increase the stimulation of the energy in that particular place. For best results, place an aquarium in the wealth sector of your home office. Goldfish are good, but avoid predatory fish.

Water and fish

Representative of life and good fortune, moving water, such as fountains and aquariums, can help stimulate positive Qi. Due to its cool and passive qualities, water also has a calming effect. In Chinese, "fish" also means "surplus" – so a fish tank with active, colorful goldfish could boost your finances. For best results, place it in the wealth sector of the home office. Make sure that fish tanks are kept clean and contain living plants and natural features. Displaying the fish symbol as a vase, sculpture, painting or on a screen is also effective – the best places for this are near the front entrance or on the living room table.

Aroma

It's important that our homes smell fresh, energized and clean. Aromatic scented oils, candles, or incense are effective, both sweetening the air and making a colorful statement. Try applying fresh potpourri, fruit or flowers. But beware of overkill – natural smells and fresh air are best. Open windows, cross-ventilate, use fly screens on windows and doors. The wonderful smells from home cooking are excellent Feng Shui, making us feel comforted and nurtured.

Sound

Wind chimes are the most common way sound is used in Feng Shui. Their song activates Qi, but can also slow it down if it is traveling too quickly through a house. As wind chimes react to small air movements, they also act as a subtle alarm to let you know someone is coming. Ticking clocks can be reassuring, gentle background music, as can the sound of birds, the ocean or bubbling water.

Sight and movement

Objects which bring light and color into an area activate positive Qi. Crystals, lighting, mirrors, bamboo flutes, mobiles, sculptures – even paintings – will enliven dark, stagnant areas. The unicorn is considered a creature of good omen, symbolizing longevity, joy and wisdom. The Chinese believe the unicorn is always solitary, appearing only when a particularly benevolent leader sits on the throne or when a wise sage is born. The peacock signifies dignity and beauty. Feathered fans are often hung in Chinese homes and for centuries were popular emblems of official rank.

Objects which flutter in the wind, such as colored ribbons or mobiles, stimulate positive Qi and deflect negative Qi. Ribbons tied to an artificial ventilation system in the bathroom will get Qi moving, and a weather vane on the roof of your home will help discourage negative Qi. Hang bamboo flutes (with a red ribbon) from an oppressive beam or beneath an archway between a front and back door which directly face each other. Hang crystals in windows or keep them in clusters on side tables.

Above: Wind chimes have many beneficial properties that can potentially enhance our environment. Their melodious sound (and other sounds such as music or bubbling water) is considered good Feng Shui, especially for shifting energies and cleansing the air. Wind chimes help define boundaries between indoor and outdoor spaces and help to moderate the flow of fast-moving Qi in long corridors. But consider whether you like the sound before you buy a chime, as you'll have to live with it!

Above: In ancient China, the dragon was the most revered celestial animal. The dragon symbolized great power, while many natural phenomena (such as droughts, storms, typhoons or floods) were explained as manifestations of the dragon's moods.

Above: Feng Shui masters advise using old Chinese coins (round coins with a square hole in the middle) to activate the wealth/prosperity sector of your home. Hanging six or eight *I Ching* coins in this sector is auspicious Feng Shui. Another method is to tie three old coins together with red thread, then attach them to your invoice or accounts book; this will attract wealth and business luck.

Above: If you're planning or buying a home, a word of Feng Shui advice is to avoid a staircase which starts directly in front of the main entrance – as the Qi created is too powerful and hard-hitting. In this instance, energy will rush straight up the stairs and be lost. Try blocking the view or slowing down Qi with plants, furniture, a tall vase of flowers, a screen or a bookcase.

Staircases, Halls, Mezzanines

Traditional harmony

STAIRCASES

A Feng Shui no-no is the staircase which starts directly in front of the front door. The Qi created is too powerful, with poison arrows rushing straight up the stairs. From the main door, staircases should be concealed from view. Similarly, avoid staircases ending directly in front of an upstairs door. Gently curving staircases are preferable to those which are straight and long; equally, they should not be too narrow nor too steep, which may make them difficult to use. Steps are best if they are solid and covered, not left exposed. Unfortunately for lovers of skeletal and minimalist staircases, the spaces between each step allow auspicious Qi to escape.

Spiral staircases are not recommended either, as their shape resembles a corkscrew piercing the heart of the house, resulting in bad Feng Shui. To diminish their effect, place them in an unobtrusive corner. The worst combination is a winding staircase carpeted in red. Also, be wary of placing the staircase in the wealth corner of the house, as it can cause financial loss.

HALLS / CORRIDORS

When we step into a home, whether it's our own or not, our first impression is of the hall. A light, spacious, brightly colored and clutter-free hall is best. A long, dark corridor which is cluttered and cramped will set the tone and feeling for the rest of the space. The Chinese believe that narrow, dark hallways can evoke feelings of depression. Be aware of the placement of long hallways or corridors in or near your home – poison arrows thrive in this territory. If home is an apartment at the end of a long hall, for example, the Qi flow will be fierce. The best remedy here is to soften and slow its effect by placing bushy plants along the corridor and near your front door.

Split-level and mezzanine floors within the home are not generally advocated by Feng Shui practitioners. If you are left with no alternative to one of these, make sure your dining area is located on the higher level. This ensures that, in accordance with Chinese principles, the Qi of the residents is higher than that of the visitors, who are entertained in the lower level living room. For similar reasons, bedrooms, family rooms and studies should never be located on the lower levels of a house.

Modern design

Should you have a staircase in view of the front door, block the view with plants, furniture, a tall vase of flowers, a screen or a bookcase. A colorful round rug or crystal chandelier will effectively gather Qi in the hall. A wind chime which sounds as the door opens will stop Qi flowing into the house too quickly.

Pay close attention to the lighting and decoration of staircases and hallways. Low ceilings can feel restrictive and make moving furniture difficult, but overcoming these problems will be worth it.

Apply bright colors and mirrors in hallways to lighten and brighten them. Coat hooks, shoe cupboards, racks, umbrella stands and wooden trunks are all effective ways to reduce clutter and can make our homecoming easier.

Break down Qi flow in long, straight corridors by using plants. If you have a spiral staircase, wrap some ivy or green silk around it and make sure a light shines from the top to the bottom. Place plants beneath staircases to ground the staircase's energy.

Far Left: Although a much sought after contemporary look, minimalist staircases constructed from steel or aluminum are bad Feng Shui – the spaces between each step allow auspicious Qi to escape.

Left: A sacred space enhancer, representing all five elements, has been applied here to ground and nurture the supportive energy and to slow down the escape of Qi in this area.

The Living Room

Traditional harmony

The living room, the most public part of the house, juggles myriad functions. It's a space to relax, discuss, entertain, listen to music, watch the daily news. Given the living room's pivotal role within our lives, its arrangement, adaptability and feeling are crucial to good Feng Shui. Where the living room has a dining or work space attached, as is the case in many modern apartments, the application of good Feng Shui becomes even more important. It's important to screen off the study or office areas, so that work is not preying on your mind while you're trying to relax.

The energy of the living room is predominantly yang, given the activity and movement within the space. To ground the energy, apply yin additions such as fabric-covered seats, scatter cushions, ottomans, muted tones or cool, leafy plants. A suitably oriented living room is one which captures the sun at the right times for those who use it – an easterly aspect is good for early risers, and a westerly aspect is good for those of us who are night owls. Generally, keep living spaces well ventilated, with lots of natural light.

Where possible, make sure the living room is not positioned at the end of a long corridor – a spot which suffers from hard-hitting poison arrows. Externally, check for sharp lines from a neighbor's roof line or telephone pole, which may produce the same effect.

Furniture is best placed against the room's four walls, and its size and shape should mirror the size and shape of the room. If the pieces are too large, the flow of Qi will be disrupted, making you and your guests feel uncomfortable. For a square room, use a square, round or octagonal table. A rectangular table is best in a rectangular room. In rooms where chairs and tables are not backed by a wall, create stability behind the seating by placing a table, screen, storage unit or bookcase there.

To encourage the free flow of movement, for people and Qi, there should be an even number of chairs, and they should be positioned appropriately. Seating a person so that their back is toward a full-length window or door will make them feel insecure, so avoid placing chairs in this position. Try to make sure that the main entrance to the room can be seen from each

Above: Having skylights which allow natural light into the living area of your home is good Feng Shui. A suitably well-oriented living room is one which captures the sun; it should have an easterly aspect for early risers and a westerly one for those of us who are night owls. Air-flow and good ventilation in any room allows positive Qi to circulate.

Opposite: The color, shape, proportion and aspect of this living room are welcoming and warm. Bookcases and wall units have been kept low, to avoid a top-heavy feeling. Against a more tonal yin backdrop, colorful and textural insertions – purple fluffy rugs, paintings and flowers – have been added for yang energy. The coffee table, couch and light are good shapes, as they produce no poison arrows. The ventilation and natural light are also good.

Above: The ideal environment for food preparation should be nurturing, warm and inspiring. Monochromatic, tonal colors don't stimulate the appetite. A staircase in close proximity to the kitchen also means that positive Qi will flow straight up the stairs and be lost.

Above: The balance of yin and yang is vital here, as two elements are at play: Fire (yang) and Water (yin). Having two opposing elements side by side – the stove (Fire) next to the sink (Water) – is undesirable. A wooden buffer has been placed between the two to diffuse and ground the energy.

Poison arrows love modern, high-tech kitchens. So avoid jutting corner cupboards, visible knives or open shelves. Qi should be able to flow freely around the kitchen. This isn't possible if the kitchen door is in line with the outside doors and windows – Qi will be channeled straight through.

Modern design

Often, modern kitchens are so "designed" they lack soul until a personal touch or theme is introduced. Remember, where you live should be a reflection of who you are, the journey you have been on, the relationships you wish to nurture. In short, your home (including your kitchen) should be filled with positive memories and future aspirations. The ideal environment for food preparation and whetting the appetite should be nurturing, warm and inspiring. Maintaining balance in the kitchen can be achieved by applying one of each of the five elements. The kitchen is already a powerful source of the Fire element (the stove), so the addition of red or orange furnishings or painted walls might be too overpowering. Instead, try incorporating a stone floor or adding stone pots for the Earth element, and add a blue tablecloth or aquarium for Water. But remember, insipid colors do little to stimulate the appetite – a lively, joyful environment is still necessary.

Placing the stove (Fire) next to the sink or refrigerator (Water) isn't good, as it's undesirable to have these two elements side by side. If you have no option but to do this, place a buffer, such as a metal or wooden partition, even a chopping board, between the two. Other options for diffusing this opposing energy in your kitchen include tribal art carved from wood, a metal sculpture, wooden salt and pepper shakers, a wooden spice box, a metal device for weighing ingredients, a cappuccino maker or an attractive stainless steel vase filled with bamboo.

Make sure the open-plan kitchen is defined by barriers such as furniture, lampshades, mobiles, color or plants. But beware of barriers being too solid. Choose light, natural materials, which can be easily stored away. Screens made from cloth, wood or woven hyacinth are a perfect option. And design the kitchen sensitively, using rounded shelves instead of square ones. Choose smooth surfaces, preferably in lighter shades. Indoor plants, window boxes or small shrubs outside the window will help the environment stay cool. Why not try potting herbs in a planter box outside your window.

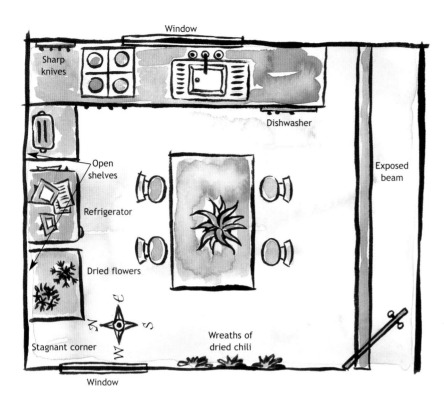

Window

Sharp knives

Dishwasher

Open shelves

Refrigerator

Dried flowers

Stagnant corner

Window

Exposed beam

Wreaths of dried chili

Planter box

Earth pots

Images of food

Window

Bad Feng Shui—Kitchen

- Stagnant corner
- Dried flowers and freestanding, open shelves create poison arrows
- Photos of old relationships and bills on refrigerator
- Sharp knives on display
- Square table in center creates poison arrows
- Spiky plant
- Stove placed beside sink (Fire and Water elements should not be placed next to each other)
- Heavy exposed beam

Good Feng Shui—Kitchen

- Earth pots have been placed on top of storage to "ground" energy
- The stove is opposite the door, with a reflective surface added behind the burner – this is good Feng Shui
- Oversized square table has been replaced with round table, with bowl of fruit and blue tablecloth
- Freestanding open shelves have been replaced with built-in, rounded shelves
- Exposed beam has been wrapped in soft fabric
- Planter box with herbs and geraniums placed outside window
- Knives have been stored away
- Chilies have been replaced with images of food to create illusion of abundance
- A wooden chopping board has been placed between stove (Fire) and sink (Water)

Above: There are two conflicting roles at work in the bathroom: Water represents money and it washes away dirt. So, flushing water in the bathroom potentially means losing wealth. Avoid locating bathrooms in any of the important wealth or career sectors of the house, since showers, toilets or baths placed in this sector will drain positive prospects and luck. Also, keep the toilet lid down and try to keep drains covered.

Bad Feng Shui—Bathroom

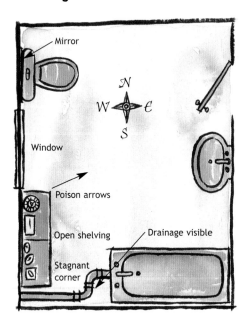

The Bathroom

Traditional harmony

Bathrooms are places of cleansing and purification, private retreats where you can escape from the world. So they should be peaceful, with soothing music, colors and aromatic oils. Good lighting is beneficial, as are cleanliness, ventilation and simplicity. The bathroom poses an interesting Feng Shui conundrum, as its basic element (Water) plays two roles – it represents money and it washes away dirt. So every time you flush water down the drain, you are in danger of sending your finances away with it.

To rectify this, avoid locating bathrooms in any of the important wealth or career sectors of the house. Showers, toilets or baths placed in this sector will drain positive prospects and luck – keep dripping taps in check. Try not to locate the bathroom in the middle of the house (Earth), as negative energy will spread from the center to all parts of the building. Instead, bathrooms should be sited along the sides of the house, tucked away discreetly.

Within the bathroom, toilets are best hidden from view; avoid facing them toward staircases or dining rooms. Toilets shouldn't be located at the end of a corridor or in the vicinity of the main door. And bathrooms, as they are associated with Water, shouldn't be next to the kitchen, which is associated with Fire – Water destroys Fire.

Bad Feng Shui—Bathroom
- The mirror above the toilet reflects the toilet and also faces the door, which is to be avoided
- The toilet is visible from the door
- No mirror or storage near sink
- The open door allows negative Qi to flow into the rest of the house
- Poor use of space between sink and bath, and bath and shelves
- Cluttered shelves
- See-through windows with slatted blinds

Modern design

If you can't avoid having the bathroom near the front door or in the center of the home, balance the energy by placing tall plants around the toilet. Placing plants where there is excess Water energy will redress the balance of the elements. Also, keep the toilet lid down, try to keep drains covered and hang a small convex mirror on the outside of the bathroom door to prevent energy going in and being lost. Other options are to install a ventilated skylight and to place colored ribbons or wind chimes near artificial ventilation devices – they will flutter, making music and enlivening Qi. Placing a small mirror at the base of the toilet also stops Qi and your wealth from going down the drain. If the toilet is near the kitchen, hang a ceramic mobile or wall plaque (Earth element) between the rooms to moderate the different energies. Try hiding the toilet with a screen, half-wall, door, alcove, curtain or cabinet.

Apply large mirrors so that they reflect as much of the person as possible – these will also increase the sense of space. The bathroom is the most yin room in the house and is often dark and damp, so add yang for balance – some bright splashes of color or lighted candles. While the use of uninterrupted color such as white is beneficial, it will need warming up. Green and blue are good Feng Shui, but also try subtle splashes of peach, red or pink. Add richness through texture – wicker, glass, ceramics or cotton. The good news for art deco fans is that black and white diamond tile floors are good for holding the energy in the room.

Finally, doors leading to bathrooms are best kept closed.

Good Feng Shui—Bathroom

- The mirror has been removed from behind the toilet
- The toilet lid is down
- A screen has been provided to block toilet from view, creating privacy
- Black and white diagonal tiles throughout to "ground" energy
- A mirror has been placed on the outside of the door, which makes the room invisible when the door is closed
- A large, framed mirror has been hung above the sink; it includes storage for toothbrushes, etc.
- A yin rug has been added
- A round table concealing the drainage has been added. Place candles, flowers, sweet-smelling oils on it. The table has a concealed shelf underneath, which reduces clutter.
- Curtains and frosted glass have been added to the windows for privacy.

Above: Placing plants where there is excess water energy will redress the balance of the elements. Large mirrors also increase the sense of space. The bathroom is the most yin room in the house, and is often dark and damp, so add yang for balance — some bright splashes of color (such as glass vases and plants, as used here) or lighted candles. Also use texture to add richness — wood, stone, glass tiles, ceramics, cotton, wicker.

Good Feng Shui—Bathroom

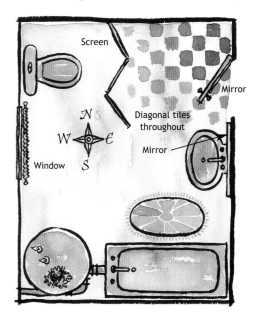

The Bedroom

Traditional harmony

The bedroom, our private sanctuary, should be honored as a place of rest, rejuvenation and romance. It's our place of retreat, for comfort and restoration. The bedroom is best when clutter free, predominantly yin and comfortable, with a décor which soothes rather than distracts.

As such, the bedroom should not be activated too heavily with Feng Shui cures. Water features are a no-no in the bedroom, as the Chinese believe they provoke bad luck and disturb sleep. Avoid indoor plants or electrical equipment such as clocks, radios, televisions; their yang energy is too invigorating for this space. Keep an eye out for generators of poison arrows – sharply angled walls or the corners of furniture pointing toward the bed. Remove them, move them or opt for rounded shapes and soothing colors instead.

The position and placement of the bed is paramount in Feng Shui. Balanced furnishings should be placed on either side of the bed, but leaving ample room to move. It is considered inharmonious to push a bed up against a wall or otherwise constrain it. Check for beams and storage overhead – both can be oppressive. Consider altering the direction of your bed so that it is in your favorable direction, with your head facing that way when you are lying down. The Chinese believe that the bed's best position is diagonally opposite the door, with an unobstructed view to the door. Avoid positioning the bed between the door and the window, or between two windows, as a line of Qi crossing the bed is thought to cause illness. Having the foot of the bed in a direct line with the door is known as the "mortuary position" in China – coffins are placed in that position when they are awaiting collection.

A window behind a headboard is bad Feng Shui, as the headboard is then unsupported, leaving the person sleeping there unprotected. A dressing room is good, as it frees the bedroom for rest and romance. A connecting bathroom door opening directly onto the bed should be avoided, as it will drain positive Qi.

Above: Used indiscriminately, the color orange may be too mentally stimulating for the bedroom. If avoiding orange proves difficult, dilute its potency by adding muted yin tones as exemplified in the bedroom above. And a word of warning: avoid peach. "Peach-Blossom Luck" is a famous concept in China, pertaining to a husband or wife with a roving eye. Apply peach in your bedroom and you're asking for trouble if you're married!

Opposite: The position and placement of the bed is paramount in Feng Shui. Furnishings that are balanced in size, proportion and color should be placed either side of the bed, still allowing ample room to move. Pushing a bed up against a wall or constraining it with bedside tables or shelves is considered inharmonious. Consider moving your bed so that it faces your favorable direction. Choose décor that soothes rather than distracts.

Modern design

Furnishings either side of the bed don't have to be identical, just balanced. Sensitively maintaining balance within the home is one of the keys to auspicious Feng Shui. Bedside tables and lamps should be of equal height, size and proportion. Try wood or woven fiber furniture, as the Metal element is too "sharp" for the bedroom. If that's not possible, cover metal furniture with a yin cloth to soften its effect. Also consider clutter: select bedside tables with drawers for storage. Apply candles to create soft pools of light, and sweet-smelling potpourri or burning oils to keep the air fresh. Scatter the bed with silk cushions or mohair throw rugs. Adorn the walls with yin-colored wall hangings, woven rugs or tapestries – but be minimal. Place a picture of you and your loved one by your bed or in the relationship sector of the room. Consult your Bagua to establish where this is positioned in your bedroom. Images of a single person may evoke feelings of loneliness, as does a single bed. Hang a red and gold "double happiness" calligraphy in this sector to strengthen your relationship or marriage.

Where possible, banish work-related objects such as date books, mobile phones and laptops. Remove piles of unread books and magazines. And select battery-operated devices such as clock radios over electrical ones – the aim is for relaxation and calm. If it's not entirely possible to remove this day-to-day hardware, at least arrange appropriate storage to conceal it at night. But remember, don't store this bric-a-brac under the bed, as this is thought to represent sleeping on issues you're not willing to face. The best spot for storage would be in an enclosed basket, a wooden chest or in the closet.

If having a view of the door proves difficult, use a mirror to reflect anyone entering. You can also use mirrors to correct the situation when a bedroom door directly faces another door. Avoid mirrors facing the bed, though, as the Chinese believe the soul leaves the body while sleeping, and it will be disconcerted if it comes across itself in the mirror. Cover mirrors with a yin-colored cloth before going to sleep. Do the same for open shelves and storage spaces.

Ideally, beds should be made of natural materials, such as wood or bamboo, and raised above the floor so that air can circulate underneath. Always purchase new pillows when moving into a new house, as they represent new beginnings and are symbolic of leaving your old problems behind.

Above: Battery-operated devices (such as this clock radio) are preferable to plugged-in electrical devices for the bedroom. Electrical devices, which also include televisions and stereos, are too yang and energetic for the bedroom, which should be predominantly yin.

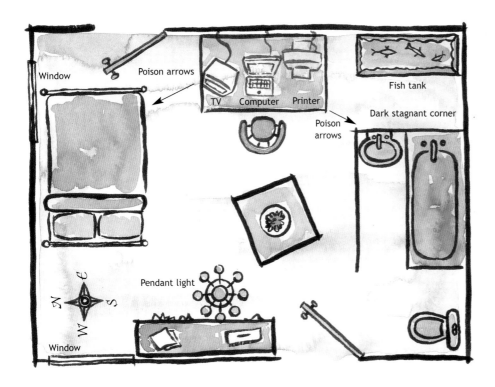

Window

Poison arrows

TV   Computer   Printer

Fish tank

Dark stagnant corner

Poison arrows

Pendant light

Window

Bad Feng Shui—Bedroom

- Windows have venetian blinds
- Unbalanced distribution of space; for example, the bed is very close to the wall
- The front door is aimed directly at the bed
- The office space and electrical items are too close to the sleeping area
- The fish tank should not be in the bedroom – it creates too much yin
- The toilet is in a direct line with the bed
- The square coffee table creates poison arrows and promotes the inauspicious flow of Qi
- The heavy pendant light presses down

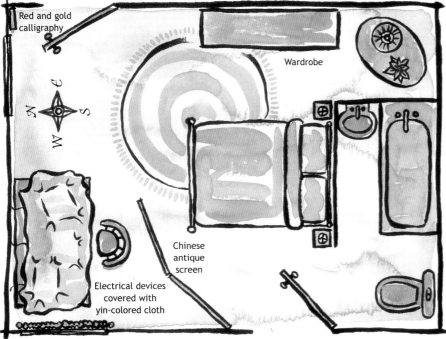

Red and gold calligraphy

Wardrobe

Chinese antique screen

Electrical devices covered with yin-colored cloth

Windows with curtains

Good Feng Shui—Bedoom

- Windows have curtains, venetian blinds have been removed
- Red and gold calligraphy is hung in corner to enhance relationships
- Chinese antique screen placed to divide sleep and work areas
- Round rug with yang colors
- Bedside tables are identical and small lamps placed either side of bed
- The bed is no longer in the coffin position, but is up against a wall for support
- An oval table with a bright lamp and plant lifts the corner
- The fish tank has been removed

Above: According to ancient Chinese tradition, attaching a Feng Shui charm such as this symbol of good fortune to a child's bedroom door will call in positive energy (Qi) and enhance the flow of peaceful energy into the room.

Above: For good Feng Shui in your child's bedroom, apply beanbags, quilts, toys and cushions with abandon. Even if the floor is concrete or wooden floorboards, provide a soft yin rug. Also remember, furniture with curved corners will not only help prevent accidents, it will also prevent poison arrows.

Children's Bedrooms

Traditional harmony

A child's bedroom serves two functions – sleep and play. So it's important to define the opposing activities through the application of positive and harmonious Feng Shui. If the application of good Feng Shui is ignored, a child may have difficulties unwinding at night. An overly yang room is too mentally stimulating for children and will affect their sleep.

As already outlined in "Color in the Home" (pages 57–65), colors play a significant role in the tone and feeling of a child's bedroom. So select shades and hues to balance the child's activities in the room. Play areas should be bright, to enhance children's learning, creativity and curiosity, and sleep areas should be decorated with soft yin colors.

More importantly, children should feel safe – so a view of the door is essential. Strange shapes and shadows lurking in dark corners can be a source of fear for children. As with adults' bedrooms, children's beds should face their supportive direction. The Chinese believe that if your child is troubled, you should use a compass to check the direction in which they are sleeping or studying. Preferably move the child's bed to face their supportive direction.

Children's beds should have a headboard and should not back onto a window or a door. If your child's bed doesn't have a headboard, make a mock-headboard by applying a colorful screen or mural, to create a sense of security and protection. Watch for beams, storage or shelves overhead – these can be oppressive. Heavy pictures on the wall behind the bed or a towering bedside light can also be oppressive. Also, bunk beds and canopies over the bed depress positive Qi.

At night, remove mirrors from your child's bedroom or cover them with a cloth. If bedroom doors are continually slammed by children, indicating that the children are trying to attract energy toward them, attach a Feng Shui ring bell charm to the inside of their door to encourage cooperation.

Modern design

The perfect way to define play/study (yang) and sleep (yin) areas in a child's bedroom at night is to cover the dominantly colored areas with yin-colored fabric or curtains. A wooden screen is also a good option for defining the opposing areas, as it creates a psychological barrier between activities. It is equally important that mirrors are covered at night. Green, purple or blue fabric is best, with tranquil or restful motifs such as fish, sea life, mermaids or flowers blowing in the wind. A soft night-light can be effective to help children relax.

Furniture with curved corners will not only help prevent accidents; it will also prevent poison arrows. Stimulate a child's sense of touch with numerous textures – furry, soft, hard, smooth. Use fluffy beanbags and cushions. If the floor is hard and cold, apply a soft yin rug.

Create fun, spacious storage options for toys and clutter, but do not store things under the bed.

In nurseries, hang a colorful mobile at the end of the bed, but not above, as this can be perceived as threatening. Bells tied to the cot can be stimulating by day, but are best removed at night. Decorate and paint the room for a new baby as long as possible before it is due, and air the room thoroughly after painting so that the paint fumes disappear. Preferably, decorate the room with natural products and use bedding made from natural fibers.

And lastly, sound is soothing and reassuring to children, so try musical mobiles or classical music to help send them to sleep.

Above: A child's bedroom serves two functions – sleep and play. So it's important to define the opposing activities through positive and harmonious Feng Shui. If this is ignored, a child may have difficulty unwinding at night. An overly yang room or play area, such as this one, is too mentally stimulating for children and will affect their sleep, if in close proximity to their bed. So either erect a screen to shield it, define the area through the use of paint or furnishings, or store playthings away at night.

The Home Office

Traditional harmony

A working or study environment in the home can be difficult Feng Shui, as the energy from these areas can affect the entire house. But, if approached correctly and sensitively, beneficial rewards can be reaped. Surplus yang energy is more likely to gather in the home office than in the study or studio, as contact with the outside world is greater. So striking a balance is imperative when planning and utilizing this space.

The home office is best located in close proximity to the front entrance; ideally, it should be a place clients have access to via a separate door. The area will be most effective if it is positioned in your best direction and if the layout is designed to facilitate the auspicious flow of Qi.

While having your home office in a completely separate building on your plot of land is positive Feng Shui, stealing some space from the living room or bedroom is often closer to reality. In the latter instance, it's imperative to keep the working environment distinct from the rest of your life. Simply installing a clear division – a screen, bookshelves, cupboards or modular storage units – will do the trick.

An office in the bedroom provides a particular Feng Shui conundrum, as the room then has the opposing requirements of rest (yin) and yang (work). Covering a printer or computer with a yin-colored fabric at night will be effective here. Also, check that your desk is not placed directly underneath a window, as the Qi flow has the potential to disturb. Placing your desk in a secure corner, with your back against the wall and the doorway clearly visible, is a safer bet.

When two people are working in the same room, their desks should not face each other. Each desk should have a wall behind it to protect it, and both people should have supportive chairs. Visiting clients should be seated in what the Chinese call the "subordinate chair," with their back to the door. The owner's chair should always be backed by the wall facing the door.

The next task is to consider the contents of the desk, either using compass directions or symbolically. Finally, lighting should be diagonally opposite the writing hand to prevent shadows.

Opposite: A plant serves two purposes in this home office. Electrical devices, such as computers, printers and scanners, are very yang, so a yin plant helps diffuse the energy. Also, since this desk is positioned close to a door, a plant serves as a protector/barrier from unfavorable Qi. It is worth noting that laptops are good Feng Shui, as they can be shut down and tucked away.

Above: Be careful with Feng Shui in the home office or study – this area's energy can affect the entire house. Appropriate filing, storage and shelving can make a big difference. Check the positioning and height of your storage – storage which is too high can be oppressive, particularly if it is over the desk.

Above: Applying Feng Shui in the home office correctly and sensitively can also reap beneficial rewards. Here a plant and soft cushion add yin energy to a mainly yang space. Clutter has been removed. A red invoice book has been stored in the fame sector. Other options include red furnishings or representations of Fire such as strong lighting – but use a delicate touch.

Modern design

Make sure your home office is clutter free, and has appropriate filing, storage and shelving. Remain aware of positioning and height of furniture – storage that is too high can be oppressive, particularly if it's over the desk, such as shelves built into a wall above the desk. If a desk is close to a door, a plant on the edge of the desk will prevent unfavorable Qi.

Check anything that will detract from the entrance – weeds, dustbins, overhanging branches. A potted plant on either side of the entrance is good Feng Shui; alternatively, protect the entrance with two stone lions (fu dogs) – these help reduce the entry of negative Qi into the building. Putting a moving water feature at or near the main door will also welcome good Qi. Make sure the entrance is lit with uplights or similar artificial lighting, which will help enhance positive energy in and around the home office. Applying a Bagua mirror outside (but never inside!) the entrance will work to deflect any negative energy entering this potentially wealth-creating space.

If the office is part of another room, define the office area by a screen, a piece of furniture, even a rug. Definition, or boundaries, psychologically defines the space and its career-oriented activities. It also allows for concentration on the task at hand. Add a soft-leafed hanging plant over bookshelves. Any poison arrows should be hidden by using mirrors or screens. The great news is that laptops are good Feng Shui, as they can be shut down and tucked away. If you own a free-standing computer monitor, simply cover it with a yin-colored cloth when not in use. Place a plant close to any of your electrical equipment (such as printers and scanners) to further diffuse yang energy.

Aspirational images, good lighting and bright colors all make a psychological impact and evoke success. A traditional Chinese Feng Shui tradition is to tie three Chinese coins together with red thread or ribbon and place them in your accounts book for good luck. Also, try activating the prosperity sector by using water features, such as fish tanks. The very best fish for attracting prosperity are Arrowanas, known in the East as the "Feng Shui fish." Activate the fame sector by installing red furnishings or other representations of Fire, such as strong lighting.

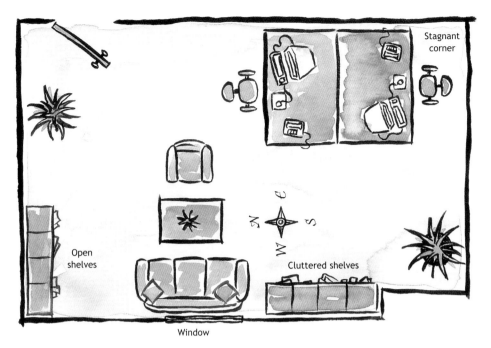

Stagnant corner

Open shelves

Cluttered shelves

Window

Bad Feng Shui—Home Office

- The open shelves are facing the seats – this is bad Feng Shui
- The spiky plants do little to break down the negative flow of Qi
- It is bad Feng Shui for colleagues to face each other all day
- The square coffee table generates poison arrows
- The window has slatted blinds, which send negative Qi into the room
- The sofa is unsupported by the window, which will cause sitters to feel uncomfortable
- There is no distinction between work and discussion zones
- The room has a bad distribution of space

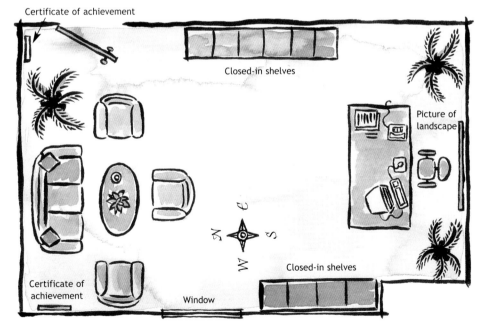

Certificate of achievement

Closed-in shelves

Picture of landscape

Certificate of achievement

Window

Closed-in shelves

Good Feng Shui—Home Office

- The sofa is supported by a wall
- The office is divided into office and discussion areas, which appropriately balances the space
- The oval coffee table does not produce poison arrows
- The window is covered with soft, flowing curtains
- The clutter-free desk is possible owing to the storage provided by the closed-in shelves
- The person seated at the desk is supported by the wall behind and is able to see the front door
- The picture of a landscape symbolically supports the back of the chair
- Soft-leafed plants are good Feng Shui – they eliminate excess yang energy

Above: Occupants of this studio apartment will feel depressed and lonely. Little consideration has been given to the sharp angles and stagnant corners of this space. The lighting and the furniture are too angular, and not in proportion to the room. There's too much yang energy and not enough cozy yin spaces.

Above: The beauty of a studio apartment is that few living functions are walled off. The Feng Shui practitioner can enhance, conceal and increase intimacy in pockets of the space by adding clusters of chairs, footstools, coffee tables – but make sure the furniture is soft, rounded, comfortable and inviting. Colorful artwork is another beneficial way of lifting the energy in a dark corner.

The Studio Apartment

Traditional harmony

In the case of the studio apartment there is a Feng Shui incongruity, as the Bagua is applied simultaneously to the whole premises and to just one room, with the entire space being segmented into eight sectors. So which aspirations to promote and which sectors to energize should be carefully considered. Energizing more than three of the eight, especially in a cramped, constrained environment, could be conflicting. Focus instead on the harmonious balance of the elements in any one sector.

In many contemporary apartments, the main door opens onto the main living area, leaving little protection from fast flowing or negative Qi. Traditionally, a screen would be erected directly inside the door to rectify or reduce the problem, but often this can be impractical. Plants or hat stands are often applied instead.

When checking which direction a studio apartment faces, go by the direction of the street door of the main building, not the door of the apartment. And be particularly careful of poison arrows, both internally and externally. Look out for urban skyline fixtures such as telephone poles, neighboring buildings or sharp, sloping roof lines.

If you are buying an apartment, be aware of communal staircases. They're preferable to staircases on the sides of the building; ideally, the staircase should not face the main door of the building or the entry to the home. Otherwise Qi will be fast flowing and potentially harmful.

A view of the water enhances the Feng Shui of any apartment building. However, pools should not be located within the apartment block, either on the ground floor or the top floor. It is believed that water above or below spells danger.

Modern design

The beauty of a studio apartment is that few living functions are walled off – this gives greater freedom to enhance the Feng Shui of certain sectors without dividing the space. A range of techniques can be applied to enhance or conceal certain areas. Lighting can be soft, colored, moody or bright. Space can be compartmentalized and barriers implied with screens, curtains, lengths of fabric, the application of color.

Within this tricky space, use mirrors carefully, as you may inadvertently extend an area considered important while minimizing another. Be careful, particularly with large mirrors. Mirrors are great for extending "missing corners," but there may not be any missing corners in the studio apartment.

As space is limited, try enhancing the space with images or artwork. Use rounded furniture where possible. Add a water feature in the prosperity sector to enhance wealth, or place images of you and your loved one in your romance sector. If practical, place a wooden, woven or delicate paper screen inside the front door to stop the negative flow of Qi. Where possible, decorate the balcony with hanging pots.

Right: This inner-city chic studio apartment, painted in monochromatic tones, allows for either yin or yang furnishings. Storage is seamlessly concealed. Lighting and a clutter-free environment keeps Qi flowing freely. A comfortable couch, floor cushions and rounded armchairs keep this space free of hard-hitting poison arrows.

Index

Acknowledgments

Thanks to the following for props and locations:

Mary Shackman (MS)
  Paddington, NSW, Australia
  shackman@iprimus.com.au
  http://home.iprimus.com.au/shackman

Zest, Bedroom Gallery & Interior Furnishings (Z)
  Moore Park Supa Centa, Kensington, NSW, Australia
  zestbedz@telstra.com

Australian Galleries
  Rolyston St, Paddington, NSW, Australia

Dinosaur Designs (DD)
  Elizabeth St, Strawberry Hills, NSW, Australia
  and Mott St, Nolita, New York, USA
  dinosaur@zip.com.au

Kathy McKinnon (KM)
  Sydney, Australia
  kathy@kmck.com.au
  http://www.bookingbusiness.com.au/kmck.pdf

Imogen Carr
  imagine54@hotmail.com

Susan Avery (SA)
  Jersey Rd, Woollahra, NSW, Australia
  avery@ozeflowers.com.au
  http://www.ozeflowers.com.au

John Baker
  Paddington, NSW Australia

Rob Brown (RB)
  Dawson Brown Architecture
  East Sydney, NSW Australia
  dba@carolinecasey.com.au

Chee Soon & Fitzgerald (CSF)
  Crown St, Surry Hills, NSW Australia
  cheesoonfitz@yahoo,com

Empire (E)
  Oxford St, Paddington, NSW, Australia
  sales@empirehome.com.au

Equator Homewares (EH)
  Glebe, NSW, Australia
  equator@ozemail.com.au

The Flower Man
  Double Bay, NSW, Australia
  www.flowerman.com.au

Heike Rewitzer Architecture and Interiors
  Surry Hills, NSW, Australia
  rewitzer@hotmail.com

Ikea
  Kensington, NSW, Australia
  www.ikea.com

Leung Wai Kee Buddhist Craft & Joss Sticks
  Trading Co.P/L (LWK)
  Pitt St, Sydney, NSW, Australia

Lynette Cunnington Chinese Art (LC)
  Queen St, Woollahra, NSW, Australia
  chineseart.mac.com

Made in Japan (MJ)
  Oxford St, Paddington, NSW, Australia
  www.mij.com.au

Simon O'Neil
  Gunlake Constructions
  Double Bay, NSW, Australia

The Orient House
  Glebe, NSW, Australia
  orienthouse@orienthouse.net.au

Orson & Blake (OB)
  Surry Hills, NSW, Australia
  orsonbl@zipworld.com.au

Ruby Star Traders
  Glebe, NSW, Australia
  sales@rubystar.com.au

Sam Crawford Architect (SC)
  Surry Hills, NSW, Australia
  samcrawford@ozemail.com.au

Siimon Reynolds (SR)
  Double Bay, NSW, Australia
  mail@lovecommunications.com.au

Spence & Lyda (SL)
  Foster St, Surry Hills, NSW, Australia
  www.spenceandlyda.com.au

Tibet Gallery (TG)
  Queen St, Woollahra, NSW, Australia

Victoria Spring (VS)
  Oxford St, Paddington, NSW, Australia
  www.victoriaspringdesigns.com

Whitecliffe Imports (WI)
  Bridge Rd, Glebe, NSW, Australia
  whitecliffe@chilli.net.au

Photo Credits

MS: 9, 40, 47, 57, 83, 87, 89; Z: 5, 6, 8, 16, 18, 22, 30, 44, 54, 56, 58, 63, 77, 94, 95; KM: 7, 17, 18, 29, 46, 51, 55, 62, 68, 70, 90, 94; DD: 9, 70, 89; SA: cover, 74; RB: 38, 67, 69, 81, 92; CSF: 46, 83; E: cover, 65, 80; EH: 3, 39, 50, 61, 84; LWK: 1, 13, 22, 26, 31, 58, 75, 79, 98, 100, 106, 108; LC: cover; MJ: 24; OB: 51, 62, 83, 90; SC: 43, 48, 49, 76; SR: 84, 86, 87, 104, 105; SL: 45; TG: cover & 18; VS: 73; WI: 4